FROM FIRE, BY WATER

SOHRAB AHMARI

From Fire, by Water

My Journey to the Catholic Faith

IGNATIUS PRESS   SAN FRANCISCO

Cover design by John Herreid

To Father R.C.J., who made Christ visible.
And to my Maximilian.

He brings down to Sheol and raises up.

—1 Samuel 2:6

CONTENTS

FOREWORD

You hold in your hands the best personal memoir I have read in many years: honest, vividly written, and compelling. Sohrab Ahmari is emerging as one of the finest minds and writers of his generation, and the story of his conversion recounted here will stay with the reader for a very long time.

This, of course, is a big claim. It requires some explanation, because today "religion" can often resemble nostalgia or sentimentalism, and the last thing Christians need is another bath in either. Stories of personal conversion are commonplace in an American culture with a taste for self-revelation, and too often the stories fail for one of two reasons: vanity lurking beneath an author's false humility, and an unseemly appetite for melodrama. The truth is, we're never as important as we think we are, and, in the end, we and our stories will be forgotten by everyone but God.

And yet, God made us social creatures for a reason. In needing each other, in depending on each other, we have a chance to learn how to love as God loves, and thereby to strengthen each other with reasons for hope. Thus we long for stories like Ahmari's—stories that ring unmistakably true and can pierce through the skepticism and disappointment that dominate our daily headlines.

One of the ironies of life is that, eventually, if we have been paying attention, we know and come to understand a great many things. This makes sense because we experience a great many things over the years and develop our skills accordingly.

But the same experiences and skills that provide us with a little wisdom and mature judgment also tend to narrow our ability to recognize new possibilities and solutions. We can become quite good at naming an illness, and explaining its nature and cause, and knowing what doesn't work, but we are not so good at imagining or bringing about a cure or a way forward. A talent at diagnosing the world still has value, because people need to wake up to the reality of a problem before they can begin to fix it. But the fixing often belongs to a different (and younger) set of eyes and skills. This is what makes authors like Sohrab Ahmari so important and also so exhilarating. They remind us that God is always young, and so are those who truly love him.

He makes all things new.

We live at a moment when science and technology can make the claims of faith seem implausible—not by attacking and disproving God but by rendering people indifferent to him, and making the vocabulary of faith incomprehensible. Yet people still suffer and die, all of us. So do the persons we care for, which means that all of us ask the question: *Why?* We long for an answer. We have a deep need for meaning. People also still love, which means that we have a need for intimacy, completion in the heart of another, and the fertility of new life. And people still have an instinct and a yearning for beauty, which means that beauty has the power to evade the blind machinery of logic and reach right into the human soul.

The Church, as Ahmari discovers in these pages, is mother and teacher, nourisher and consoler, in all of these things, and all of these things prevent human affairs, no matter how confused, from becoming permanently *inhuman*. Saint Augustine, whose own conversion took place at an age and in a climate not so different from Ahmari's, would remind us that history is the great destroyer of human illusions and vanities. But it is also the great well-spring of personal and ecclesial hope. While we mustn't be captured by the world, we very much need to love all the great good in it, serving the people who inhabit it and inviting them to the knowledge and love of Jesus Christ. We should never underestimate the power of personal witness, because without a living example of love that people can see and follow, truth is mute and sterile.

What we do as individual believers thus resonates beyond our own lives because our personal witness shapes others, and each of us as a child of God is meant to experience joy *forever*. Likewise what we do as communities of Christian friendship matters just as powerfully, because the Church, as a family of families, shapes cultures, creates the future, and sustains God's presence in the world.

Léon Bloy, the great French Catholic convert, liked to say that, in the end, the only thing that matters is to be a saint. If we are willing to listen, the Church has many good reasons why people should believe in God, and in Jesus Christ, and in the beauty and urgency of her own mission. But she has only one *irrefutable* argument for the truth of what she teaches: the personal example of her saints. This is the vocation she intends for all of us.

I found myself highlighting passages in this book that I will return to many times in the months and years ahead, but among the best of them appears on the first page of the very first chapter:

> My native land [Iran] smelled of dust mingled with stale rosewater. There was enjoyment in Iran and grandeur of a kind, to be sure. But when it wasn't burning with ideological rage, it mainly offered mournful nostalgia. Those were its default modes, rage and nostalgia. I desired something more.

The lesson here is simple. We are each created for "something more", and our hearts are restless until we find it. It is our great good fortune that Sohrab Ahmari did.

+Charles J. Chaput, O.F.M. Cap.
Archbishop of Philadelphia

PREFACE

It was a classic *Onion* headline: "Reason Man Turning to Religion Later in Life Must Be Horrifying".

The satirical news item concerned Paul D'Amato, a small-town Pennsylvania man who had suddenly taken up a life of Christian piety in late middle age. Formerly non-religious, he now attended multiple services weekly, wore a cross, and regularly brought up Christ's redeeming light in everyday conversation. The accompanying stock photograph showed a man in a plaid shirt kneeling in the pews of an empty church, his eyes shut, hands clasped in prayer.

"Boy, you've got to think it was something pretty terrible that made him religious at this point," coworker Jessica Redmond told the *Onion*'s "reporter". She went on: "The guy's nearly 50, and *now* he finds God right out of the blue? I bet it's something with drugs. Or maybe he killed someone in a car accident. Either way, something super messed up happened to him." Only something "really, really bad" could have brought about a conversion like this.

Like all good satire, the *Onion* article reflected the spirit of the age in exaggerated form. In our age, a conversion like D'Amato's appears, by turns, alarming and ridiculous. Cosmologists today can pinpoint the age of the universe down to the smallest unit of time, neurologists trace every desire to the firing of synapses in the brain, cars drive themselves, and the Internet offers total, instantaneous knowledge about nearly everything. Perhaps there is a Great Mathematician out there, our contemporaries allow,

and perhaps this deity looks upon the cosmos with a generally benign countenance. But a personal God, who takes
an interest in the destiny of Paul D'Amato of Stroudsburg,
Pennsylvania—you can't be serious.

If you *are* serious about your conversion, then it must
be owing to some trauma: drug addiction, guilt over a
past misdeed, anxiety associated with rapid globalization. Or maybe you are lonely. Maybe you are desperate
for attention.

When that *Onion* article appeared, on December 2,
2016, I was thirty-one years old and less than three weeks
away from being received into the Roman Catholic
Church. The joke cut close to the bone. I knew what it
was like to submit the contents of one's inner life for external inspection as a convert. My mostly secular friends were
more generous than D'Amato's, though in social gatherings there were the knowing smiles, the condescending
glances, and, very rarely, the expressions of outright hostility to Catholicism.

Only in my case the worldly stakes were somewhat
higher. I was working at the time in London as a column-
ist and editorial writer for the *Wall Street Journal*. More
important, I had been born and raised in the Islamic
Republic of Iran. My spiritual life was therefore laden
with political and even geopolitical weight that our fictional friend didn't have to carry. It didn't help that I had
already announced my decision to convert on the Internet.

When I began my course of instruction six months
earlier with a priest in London, I resolved not to "come
out" as Catholic until after I was baptized. In July 2016,
however, something ghastly happened across the English
Channel. A pair of jihadists inspired by the Islamic State
assailed a church in Normandy, France, and murdered a
priest, Father Jacques Hamel, while he was celebrating

Mass. They forced Father Hamel to his knees and cut his throat, but not before the old priest managed to shout: "Get away, Satan!"

The news accounts and online images of the frail and gentle Father Hamel gripped me. As a Catholic-to-be, I had to react to this atrocity. But how? I blurted out a message of solidarity on Twitter. "#IAmJacquesHamel," I wrote, in the style of the #JeSuisCharlie Twitter hashtag that became popular in the aftermath of the January 2015 Islamist massacre at the offices of the French satirical magazine *Charlie Hebdo*.

Then the big news: "In fact, this is the right moment to announce I'm converting to Roman Catholicism."

The tweet went viral. Thousands of social media users worldwide "retweeted" and "liked" the announcement or otherwise contacted me directly on Twitter and Facebook. Save for the odd fundamentalist Protestant warning me to beware the "whore of Babylon"—that is, the Catholic Church—the responses were positive. Even so, I had to delete the tweet later the same day. I was unprepared for the brouhaha it set off.

Catholicism was the destination I reached after a long, circuitous spiritual path. That path cut across my Muslim background and Iranian heritage, to be sure, and these in turn shaped its course. But it wasn't as if I had been praying to Allah one day and the next day accepted Christ as my savior. My Internet cheer squad craved precisely this simplistic narrative, which Twitter, with its tendency to flatten human experience into readily digestible memes, supplied.

As the hours went by, Christian outlets published stories about my conversion in half a dozen languages, though most didn't bother to contact me first. "Moslem Writer Moved by Priest's Martyrdom to Convert to Catholicism" was a typical headline. Still more social-media users shared these articles on their timelines, usually along with Tertullian's saying that the "blood of martyrs is the seed of the church." The narrative took on a life of its own. At first, I tried to contact the editors to request correction or clarification. I wasn't "Moslem", dammit! My conversion process had begun long before Father Hamel's killing. Eventually I grew exhausted and gave up; the online frenzy died down.

I hadn't taken stock of the public, political facets of faith. Whether I liked it or not, many people were bound to view my conversion as a decisive step from the House of Islam into Christendom. These terms sound grating to contemporary liberal ears. Liberalism honors religious faith as one of the pillars of civil society, at best, but it goes no further: The content of religion and the individual conscience are supposed to be beyond the reach of the liberal state (whether actually existing liberal governments fulfill this promise is a different story).

The trouble is that Islam makes no such distinctions between the subjective and objective sides of faith. And Catholicism—Rome—is linked with community, nationhood, and civilizational boundaries in a way that is simply not the case with the various Protestant strands of Christianity. Add the martyrdom of a French priest at the hands of radical Islamists, and you can see how I was in over my head.

* * * * *

The tweet had been a mistake. Conversion is foremost a matter of the individual conscience, and the Catholic Church's cosmic mission is the salvation of souls; everything else flows from that. In my case, however, the political currents generated by the announcement risked overtaking this more crucial interior dimension. Only a fool or an opportunist would make a public conversion like mine as a statement about Islam and Christendom. I don't believe I was either.

I became Catholic after concluding that Catholicism is true. My accidental circumstances—Muslim born, Iranian American—were secondary. How could I permit my conversion to be reduced to politics and identity, when in fact it had been sparked by the opposite idea: that there is such a thing as truth, truth that is eternal and universal and isn't circumscribed by politics, history, genetics, language, geography, or identity?

Then there was the vulgar triumphalism in some of the initial coverage. I didn't convert publicly to score a point for Team Jesus against Team Muhammad, but that was how some were interpreting my decision. If I was reacting against anything, it was against the materialism and relativism that had taken root in the West beginning in the nineteenth century. I had turned my back against Marx, Nietzsche, and Foucault, not the prophet Muhammad, whose religion had left only faint imprints on my soul by the time I entered adulthood. This was lost on many of those who applauded as I crossed the Tiber.

The hardest question raised and left unanswered by my tweet and subsequent efforts to explain myself was: Why Catholicism? The ranks of Iranian Christians have been swelling lately. Despite intense repression meted out by the ruling mullahs, there are up to a million converts in Iran, though more conservative estimates put the figure between three hundred thousand and five hundred thousand. Most of these new Christians are evangelicals. There are Catholics in the Islamic Republic, but they belong to Iran's historic Christian minorities, mainly Armenians and Assyrians. Catholicism is thus an ethnic phenomenon and relatively inaccessible for most Shiite Iranians. It is the evangelicals who, at great personal risk, distribute the Gospels in Persian and promise an immediate, personal relationship with *masih*, the Messiah.

So, again, why Catholicism? The suddenness of my turn to the Roman Church puzzled and, in some cases, disappointed evangelical friends. Was it the intellectual's snobbery that had drawn me to Catholicism? Had I fallen for "bells-and-smells" liturgy? Had I given "reformed" Christianity a fair shake before ruling it out in favor of Rome?

Meanwhile, a few of my more secular friends wondered out loud if I wouldn't have been better off with one of the mainline Protestant denominations. How could I reconcile my self-proclaimed classical liberalism with Rome's hard teachings on divorce, homosexuality, the ordination of women, and the like? The question lurking behind these questions, I suspect, was this: Had I found in the Catholic faith a way to express the reactionary longings of my Persian soul, albeit in a Latin key?

The memoir you are holding attempts to answer these questions and to correct the record—to demonstrate that my conversion was sincere, well considered, and in line with the dictates of my conscience; that my becoming Catholic had *something* to do with being Iranian- and Muslim-born but that it was ultimately a response to the universal call of grace. It retraces the steps that took me from the strident atheism and materialism of my Iranian and American youth to the small chapel in central London, where I was received into the Catholic Church on December 19, 2016.

Most of the book recounts how I came to assent to a personal God from a position of unbelief. That was the barrier I rammed against, over the course of many years, before it gave way. From there to "mere Christianity"— C.S. Lewis' term for the basic beliefs shared among the major denominations—was relatively easy going. The final leg, to Rome, was easier still. The book reflects this three-stage dynamic.

This isn't a general autobiography. The book deals with the pieces of my intellectual and spiritual life that had a bearing on my decision. It singles out a number of awakenings, if you will, a few of them concrete events, most having to do with the life of the mind. This has resulted in some elisions. There are episodes in my life that perhaps deserve to be recounted in print but that don't belong in a spiritual memoir.

The various stages of one's spiritual life don't come neatly, one after another. Nor is there some hidden device in the soul that sounds an alarm at pivotal moments, as if to proclaim: You are learning something profound here—etch this one in your mind for future reference. Spiritual growth proceeds in fits and starts, the various stages overlap, and there is much regression and backtracking. The pivotal moments seem that way only in retrospect, often after the passage of time has eroded their luster. Yet the constant temptation in a memoir like mine is to lend interior developments greater cohesion and clarity than they first possessed. I haven't always resisted this temptation, but I have tried to capture some of the turbulence, haphazardness, and essential mystery of the process.

The book, finally, touches on the lives of others—my wife, parents, grandparents, teachers, colleagues, friends, and ex-friends, who didn't necessarily ask to play characters in my memoir, and some of whom are no longer alive. I ask these others for forgiveness, and in some cases, I have changed names to protect their privacy. Paul D'Amato, I think, would understand how awkward all this can be. This is how the *Onion* concluded its fake-news report about his conversion: "At press time, speculation about

D'Amato's circumstances had grown more rampant after sources confirmed he had volunteered to read a passage from Ephesians about forgiveness and redemption during last week's services."

I feel you, Paul D'Amato.

CHAPTER ONE

"You Brought the Imam with You"

I thought I was an American before I ever set foot in the United States. When I first arrived in my adopted homeland, just before I turned fourteen, I spoke English fluently, with an American accent I had picked up from the movies. If I suffered the exile's sense of loss, I don't remember it. For while still living in the ayatollahs' Iran, I had given myself over to the American Idea. The journey across the Atlantic ratified what I had already concluded in my heart.

First, I concluded that what was Western was preferable to the non-Western. As a child, I could observe this basic civilizational fact in the packaging of any Toblerone bar, with its clean lines and rational dimensions, the outer layer of sturdy paper and the inner one of foil that crackled and gently ripped when the chocolate pyramids were broken apart. I could smell Western superiority in the synthetic aromas that clung to relatives who had traveled abroad and to their belongings. How I loved that sweet department-store scent of my grandparents' suitcase when they returned from one of their yearly trips to "the other side", to the West!

My native land smelled of dust mingled with stale rosewater. There was enjoyment in Iran and grandeur of a kind, to be sure. But when it wasn't burning with ideological rage, it mainly offered mournful nostalgia. Those

were its default modes, rage and nostalgia. I desired something more.

Early on I intuited the philosophy of Jim Dixon, the
professor protagonist of Kingsley Amis' novel *Lucky Jim*—
namely, that "nice things are nicer than nasty ones." The
West was most definitely *nice*, judging by its artifacts.
The adults in my life generally agreed, and although these
were lean years, I never lacked for Western-made toys
and treats. But no one I knew ever pushed this love to its
logical terminus, as I did.

When I got a little older my taste in things Western
expanded to culture. I was an only child, and a lonely
one, so I spent a lot of time locked up in my room with
movies, music, and books, especially the illustrated kind.
There were the boy reporter Tintin and his dog Snowy,
who careered around the world solving mysteries; Asterix,
Obelix, and their tiny Gallic village that resisted Caesar's
yoke with the help of a magic potion that lent them super-
human strength; the Little Prince of Antoine de Saint-
Exupéry; and many others of the kind.

The most enchanting stuff came from America. The
atmosphere in Iran was stultifying. Islamic conformity was
enforced on pain of death. Desperate for an escape, Iranians
of my parents' milieu—middle class, educated, urbane—
sought escape in the things that the mullahs reviled the
most: American movies and U.S. "cultural arrogance".

My family was typical in this regard, but again I took
things further than others did. In the dream worlds of Stan
Lee, Walt Disney, George Lucas, Steven Spielberg, and the
like, I glimpsed a vision of human possibility. A problem
presented itself to the Hollywood (or comic book) hero,
who then, through ingenuity, pluck, or sheer physical
might, overcame it. What a contrast this narrative structure
presented to the fatalism that imbued Iranian mythology,

in which misfortune was written into the hero's blood and no one ever overcame the Workings of Destiny!

In the Western imagination, moreover, the individual mattered as an individual. Again, by contrast, the emblem of the Iranian sensibility was the young boy who, during the war with Iraq, had strapped himself with grenades and dashed under an incoming enemy tank. To earn his spot on giant murals around Tehran and have his story recounted on state television, the model boy had consummated his devotion to nation and regime in this one irrevocable act of self-negation.

Can you blame me for preferring Luke Skywalker and Indiana Jones?

The Iranian way was irrational. It wasn't modern. "Rational" and "modern" were my watchwords from a very young age. I had fuzzy notions of what these terms meant, but this merely magnified my enthusiasm for them. If the Western way was better than the non-Western, then America was best of all. America was the vanguard of Western-ness. The fact that our leaders constantly denounced the evils of "Vaa-shang-ton" was sure proof of this. America stood at the forefront of the modern and the rational, and that was where I belonged.

If you had told me, before I set out, that decades later I would find the heart of the West somewhere entirely different—in events that took place on a dusty, blood-stained hilltop on the outskirts of ancient Jerusalem—I would have cackled in disbelief.

* * * * *

My family was essentially unhappy, but my childhood was a happy one, even magical, notwithstanding the bombings and revolutionary terror that convulsed the world beyond our doorstep—and the discord and turmoil inside.

I grew up in my maternal grandfather's house. Baba Nasser, as he was called, was a natural tinkerer. He would make gardening hats out of cardboard packaging, writing desks out of random two-by-fours, clocks out of papier-mâché—all sorts of household objects that other people purchased ready-made, my grandfather built with his hands. He was also an incorrigible hoarder. If he happened upon a rusty nail on a sidewalk, he would pick it up gently, as if he were rescuing a wounded sparrow, wrap it in a napkin, and slip it into a side pocket. Once home, he would deposit the nail into the drawer he maintained as a sort of Home for Lost Nails. There were similar homes for broken staplers, misshapen paper clips, and sundry nuts and bolts.

The two-story he built, in an old neighborhood in central Tehran, was his ultimate tinkering project. It was a large estate, with a flat roof and concrete walls. He planted flowers in the low, narrow troughs of soil that lined the exterior, to enliven the off-white facade. There were roses and lavenders, jasmines and sunflowers. A walled garden and garage divided the house and the neighboring three-story that abutted it on one side; on the other sides the house stood free. Ivies covered the garden and climbed the neighbor's wall. A persimmon tree rose above the ivies, absorbing the sun's rays and refracting streaks of red and orange when it bore fruit.

The main entrance gave way to a vestibule and stairwell that in turn led to two identical apartments, one on each floor. The units followed more or less identical plans. There was a long, narrow corridor with two bedrooms on each side. The expansive living area and dining room were situated at one end of this corridor, while the other end opened up to the garden.

Baba Nasser and my grandmother—we called her Maman Farah—occupied the ground-floor unit. Their apartment was decorated to Maman Farah's superior taste, with ornate furniture and stately wallpaper. Baba Nasser could hoard all he wanted, but under the terms of a long-standing entente with his wife, he was required to confine his knickknacks to his personal office.

My grandfather was a civil servant in the National Iranian Oil Company, then as now the most vital economic institution in the country. Maman Farah chipped in her earnings as an Arabic-language teacher at an elite girls' school. In fact, her salary was gradually overtaking his—astonishing, given that she belonged to the first generation of Iranian women to enter the labor market. This, combined with her forceful, sometimes mercurial, personality, meant that their marriage didn't always adhere to the patriarchal pattern that prevailed in Iran.

Things were good. Baba Nasser and Maman Farah took regular vacations. They maintained multiple cars. They hired all sorts of help, including at one point a chauffeur. Then life struck them with a one-two punch from which they never quite recovered. I hadn't yet been born when these events took place. But they indelibly marked my life.

* * * * *

First came the catastrophe of 1979. That was the year Iranians overthrew the shah's benign autocracy and replaced it with the Ayatollah Khomeini's Islamist regime. Baba Nasser was a victim of this act of national folly as well as a two-bit participant, for he, the mild civil servant, had imbibed the revolution's ideas. He had chanted "Allahu Akbar" from his rooftop by night and marched in the streets by day.

Talk about ingratitude. Baba Nasser's prosperity was a testament to reforms enacted by Mohammad Reza Shah

Pahlavi and his father, Reza Shah. The two Pahlavi mon-
archs had forged a modern state out of the detritus of the
Persian Empire. They gave the country stable borders,
roads and universities, a professional civil service, a modern legal code. An Iranian middle class had emerged, and
my grandparents were climbing its upper ranks as the revolution began.

"We will lose all of this."
"You don't know what you're toying with."
"Talk of an 'Islamic republic' is nonsense."
"Do you really think Khomeini will play nice with the
    likes of you? Fools!"

So warned many of our relatives. There were several coun-
terrevolutionaries in the family, as I would later learn (for,
as I say, I was born after these events transpired). Some
had served the shah's security apparatus or were otherwise
connected to the *ancien régime*. Others simply had greater
political foresight. Baba Nasser wouldn't pay heed. He had
no brief for political Islam as such, though he did grow
more pious in the years after the revolution. He notably
gave up drinking alcohol and wearing ties. Abstinence
was mandated by law under the new dispensation, while
Western neckwear was frowned upon; ties were a symbol
of decadence.

    The main force animating his worldview was nation-
alism. His father, my great-grandfather, had taken part in
the Constitutional Revolution at the turn of the twentieth
century, and he was later elected to the Majlis, or par-
liament, that came about as a result. But constitutionalism didn't take to Iranian soil. Instead of liberty, it yielded
license and chaos. Baba Nasser came to see his father's failure, and everything else he didn't like about the state of

national affairs, as the work of nefarious foreigners, especially the cunning, foxlike English.

Baba Nasser was born in 1927. Various imperial powers at the time treated Iran as a plaything. They kept the country indebted and willfully breached its borders when it suited their geopolitical ends. Predatory concessions gave the lion's share of profits from developing Iranian oil to British firms. Communist subversion hatched in Moscow was also a real threat. Baba Nasser's suspicion of foreigners wasn't entirely irrational. But over the years it had hardened into a paranoid history of the world, in which Iranians or Muslims had invented everything that was worthwhile, only to have their ideas and resources pillaged by the West. Thus, he saw the shah's pro-Western diplomacy, not as sound Cold War policy, but the vilest treachery.

My grandfather was hardly alone in viewing Iranian history as a long chain of humiliations suffered at the hands of outsiders, going back to Alexander the Great's conquest of Achaemenid Persia. Rare is the Iranian who *hasn't* been nursed on 2,500 years of grievance. The old man who detects a hidden British hand behind every petty mishap—the missing tobacco, the broken teapot—is a stock character of Persian comic literature. Iranians laugh at him without recognizing themselves in him.

In the slogans of 1979—"Independence, Freedom, Islamic Republic!" and "Neither West nor East!"—old-school nationalists like my grandfather heard echoes of earlier constitutional battles. Yet they couldn't explain what freedom would mean to a regime based on the precepts of Shariah law. Nor did they ask how Khomeini would square republicanism with his doctrine of the guardianship of the jurist, according to which a Shiite cleric was to guide the nation as supreme leader. The tide of enthusiasm swept away all doubt.

The scale of these fellow travelers' miscalculation became apparent after the revolution's triumph. Immediately, Khomeini laid the foundations of a total state. He outlawed political parties, purged the institutions, dismantled independent labor unions, and summarily executed his erstwhile leftist and secular allies. The hijab became mandatory for women. Dancing, drinking, foreign movies and music, and most other forms of fun were now strictly proscribed. The revolution didn't bring Iranians the popular sovereignty they craved, and it robbed them of the social and individual liberties they retained under the former regime.

The new Iran was a land of conspiracies and denunciations, wild utopian fantasies and pervasive dysfunction, where each day began and ended with the litany of names of the newly executed enemies of the revolution, barked out on state radio by men with mad foghorn voices. My grandfather was too moderate and mannered to thrive among the bearded fanatics who ruled this new country. His wife fared worse. Naturally blond and blue-eyed, and never as psyched for the revolution as Baba Nasser had been, Maman Farah found herself sidelined at the school where she taught, and insulted on the streets. Once, while she and Baba Nasser were out strolling, a young revolutionary ran up to them, screaming: "Go home, dirty Yanks!" The young man apologized profusely when he realized that my grandparents were Iranian, but they got the message all the same.

Yet Baba Nasser never could admit that the revolution had been a blunder. Instead, he shrank into his hobbies. When he wasn't fooling around with his gimcrack inventions, he spent hours transcribing thousand-year-old Persian manuscripts on astronomy and mathematics into modern type, to prove, once and for all, that Iranians had originated all the pivotal scientific insights that the Western usurpers claimed for themselves.

* * * * *

My grandparents' other great disappointment was their daughter's marriage—which is to say, the union that produced me.

Baba Nasser and Maman Farah had two children, a son and a daughter. Their son (my uncle) they sent to study in the United States shortly before the revolution, and he settled in Utah and took an American wife afterward. Their daughter stayed in Iran, to study abstract expressionist painting at university and, naturally, to find a husband.

As a young woman, my mother, Niloofar, was sweet tempered, mild to a fault, and something of a great beauty. But I think she was one of those daughters who struggle all their lives to win independence from their mothers.

My grandmother, you will recall, was a capable matriarch. Maman Farah knew how to cook the full repertoire of traditional Persian recipes; how to host big parties; how to juggle career and home life; and how to cultivate people who might be of help to the family, essential in a society that runs on favors. Maman Farah couldn't bear to see her daughter stumble in any of these areas. Rather than permit my mother to emerge as a full woman in her own right, she stepped in to help wherever she saw shortcomings. Maman Farah's love was fierce—and suffocating.

When my mother was twenty, a suitor turned up in the form of a brash architect with olive skin, an eagle nose, eyes hinting of mischief. He was seven years her senior. A family friend made the introduction, and though there had been other proposals that went nowhere, my grandparents instantly approved this one. It was understood that the new couple would move into the upstairs apartment following nuptials. There was too much uncertainty to let the children live alone, Maman Farah figured, what with the new regime throwing the country into one crisis after another.

My parents never had to accept full responsibility for supporting themselves, since they knew that they would always have a comfortable roof over their heads, and Maman Farah and Baba Nasser would be there to pick up the slack if they shirked their duties. This intergenerational arrangement wasn't without its benefits. It might have worked if my father had more conventional ideas about family life. But there was very little about Parviz Ahmari that was conventional.

He was one of six children of Buick Ahmari, a painter and calligrapher of some renown who, among other things, had introduced the pop-art style to Iran. The family hailed from Iran's northwestern provinces and belonged to the Azeri (Turkish) minority. Azeri was the first language in my father's house, and his parents and siblings spoke Persian with a distinct Azeri accent. My father had worked strenuously to shed the accent; not a trace of it was left when he entered adulthood.

But he didn't shed some of his father's coarser, provincial ways. "Apa", as the old painter was addressed in the Turkish manner, had a violent, unpredictable temper. His wife (my grandmother) was a sad and mousy woman, as might have been expected. She spent her time either toiling in the kitchen or else tiptoeing around the minefield that was her husband's ego.

Apa was a strict vegan and preferred raw to cooked food, believing this to be the secret to longevity. His notions on diet and digestion were the cause of interminable disputation among the Ahmaris. His dilapidated flat, in a working-class neighborhood of Tehran, permanently gave off a septic smell, because for some eccentric reason or other he refused to repair a broken toilet in the guest bathroom.

His place also brimmed with beautiful objects: works of calligraphy by Apa and other masters; miniature paintings in the classical Persian style; rococo pictures of cherubs and plump society ladies; cigarette holders, snuffboxes, and jewelry cabinets inlaid with fine marquetry. Under Apa's roof, beauty and aesthetic order contended permanently with disorder and decay.

Much the same could have been said about my father. He possessed an intuitive visual and spatial sense, which he had honed at the University of Tehran's prestigious architecture faculty. He also had a strong hand for drawing and drafting. He would have none of the hesitant, shaky lines employed by many artists as they tried out new ideas. The line should be bold, he thought. It should come from a place of manly confidence. "Better to be definite and wrong than to pussyfoot around with the pencil," he would say. He had read widely and was blessed with a quick and capacious mind. He could be immensely witty. It was this side of him that made my father such a good match for my mother.

But there was another side, a sensuous self-indulgence that left my father utterly incapable of restraining his passions. When he ate, he chewed and swallowed with such fervor that you would have thought he had never been fed. If alcohol was served at a social gathering, he would be the guest draining the last of the bottles and rummaging the cupboards for more. When he argued—whether over politics or architecture or any quotidian matter—his voice invariably rose. He smoked incessantly, three packs a day, at least. He would wake up in the middle of the night to

smoke, and fall asleep with his cigarette still lit. His bedding was riddled with burn holes.

My parents wed in 1982. My father planned a no-frills
ceremony and reception—business casual for him, an ordi-
nary dress for my mother, only a handful of very close
friends invited. Formality and tradition were to him so
much bourgeois humbug. Afterward, he refused to report
for military conscription. It is hard to blame him, since
the hellish Iran-Iraq War was raging at the time. But as an
architect, he wouldn't necessarily have been sent to the
front. And his in-laws time and again offered to leverage
their connections to settle the issue for him.

"Parviz dear," Maman Farah would tell him, "you'll
show up a few days a week. You'll sit at a desk. It'll all be
over in six months. No more conscription headache."

"Yes, yes, of course. Later, later."

But he never got around to it, mainly because he
couldn't be bothered with the bureaucratic hassle and
chose to live below the legal radar. My father was an invisible man of sorts. He couldn't vote, open a bank account,
even purchase a plane ticket. As far as he was concerned,
though, it was everyone else who was going about things
the wrong way.

"Come, come," he would say. "People destroy themselves because they forget to live in the moment." He had
a talent for justifying indolence as a matter of high philo-
sophic principle.

My mother went along. Partly it was because she had
similar ideas, and partly because she had a ductile soul that
took the shape of any stronger personality with which it
came into contact. Such antibourgeois attitudes were in
vogue among most of my parents' friends in the wild
1970s and well into the '80s. The difference was that, as
my parents grew older, most of their friends concluded

that bourgeois stability beats bohemian drift. My parents stuck to their free-spirited ways, even as the price steadily climbed.

* * * * *

My childhood cast of mind, with its clarity and mania, I owed to this odd mélange of personalities. I was born exactly six years to the day the Ayatollah Khomeini returned from his Parisian exile to herald the Islamic Republic. The coincidence was the subject of a running a joke in the family. When I was a boy, one of our relations, a gregarious retired police colonel, would ask me at every get-together: "When were you born, Sohrab?"

"February first," I would say, playing along, for of course he knew the answer.

"Pfft-pfft," he would reply, holding his nose. "You brought the imam with you"—meaning Khomeini. The Old Colonel loathed the new regime and, indeed, Islam itself.

The punch line didn't need explanation, because everyone deplored the mullahs (everyone, that is, except Baba Nasser, who tried valiantly to keep his faith in his country if not in the revolution). Yet no one dared to voice even mild opposition in public, let alone mock the supreme leader, who was revered as a quasi-messianic figure. That same Old Colonel would take the greatest care to ensure that his opinions didn't travel beyond our family.

He simultaneously lived two sets of lives, and not just when it came to politics. It was whispered knowledge in the family that the Old Colonel and his wife were fond of poker. Under the shah, gambling had been legal, and the monarch himself owned half of the casinos in Tehran. After the revolution, the Old Colonel continued to gamble, even though the new regime banned all games of chance. Only, now he and his wife played in secret, with a select group of individuals whose discretion was beyond reproach.

All Iranians had to perfect the art of living double lives in those days. Parents had to be especially cautious. Children, as everyone knows, like to spill the beans on what their parents say and do, a source of amusement and embarrassment for mothers and fathers everywhere. But under a revolutionary regime that tried to surveil and control citizens' private lives, to fashion a sort of *homo Islamicus*, a child's loose lips could sink lives. Childish curiosity called on parents to balance candor against self-preservation.

"What is that bitter, bitter stuff that you drink? Why mustn't I talk about it?" I remember asking my mother such questions all the time.

A less conscientious parent might have snapped: "Mama probably shouldn't drink wine, and you definitely aren't going to—end of discussion!" But my parents were different. They took my questions seriously and tried to offer cogent answers. My father was particularly emphatic on this point, because to him the worst offense was to insult anyone's intelligence, including a five-year-old's.

Thus, in response to my question, my mother might have explained: "We drink this grown-up drink, because we have drunk it in our family for a very long time."

"Why have you done that?"

"Because we enjoy it. When you get older, you might try it, too, and see if you like it."

"But what about the law?"

"The law in our country says otherwise now, but we disagree with the law."

I can't say that I learned to distinguish between morality and law thanks to such discussions. That came much later. But I did learn that one could deliberate over right and wrong, that it was permissible to have private reservations about public rules.

My parents were excessively lenient by Western standards, let alone Iranian ones. For one thing, they encouraged me to address them by their first names, Parviz and Niloofar. I have yet to meet anyone, Iranian or otherwise, for whom this was the norm growing up. But my parents wanted me to see myself as their coequal friend or some such. Terms like "Dad" and "Mom" or "Pa" and "Ma" were redolent of formality.

I had a huge room to myself in the upstairs apartment of Baba Nasser's house, and I could draw whatever I wished on one of the walls. When there were parties, I was free to mingle with the guests as I pleased. When we visited other people's homes, I would be granted an exemption from the kids' table and invited to dine with the adults. Since I hated plastic ware, thinking it somehow childish and beneath me, my Armenian nanny would see to it that I was served in china, unlike the other kids.

At kindergarten, I didn't have to lie down with the other children at nap time. Instead, my parents demanded that I be allowed to read, according to my preference. The teachers were flabbergasted when one day, during "song time", I stood up to protest: "What is this kiddie play? Let's hear some *real* music!" (I liked classical Persian music at home.) When I drew caricatures of my parents' friends that distilled their personalities—a bossy colleague of my father's dressed up as a goofy general—I received praise instead of rebuke.

These liberties and privileges gave me a certain self-assurance. I also developed an early taste for the life of the mind, because I had regular access to the artists and intellectuals whom my parents counted as friends. Away from the kids' table, I could hear the adults discuss the Spanish architect Santiago Calatrava's latest building or that new movie

by the dissident Iranian auteur Bahram Beyzaie. I absorbed
this elevated talk daily, even if I didn't understand most of
it. I learned the Persian word *roshan-fekr*—"intellectual",
literally "enlightened thinker"—much too soon.

I lacked the wisdom and experience that separate pre-
cocious children from thoughtful adults, but I had an
uncanny knack for mimicking maturity. I could sit at table
with my grandparents and their friends, for example, and
opine with gusto on current affairs. "The Japanese economy is surely overheating," I might have said, regurgitat-
ing something I had heard on the radio. It was obvious
that I had no idea what I was talking about, but my com-
posure delighted grown-ups all the same.

The downside to *roshan-fekr* parenting, especially with
an only child, was that it fueled my pride and selfishness. I
was sensitive. I wanted to be "good". But I came to associ-
ate being good with wowing adults. This blunted my curiosity somewhat and left some of my raw talents uncooked.
What could any adult teach me, after all, when my first
priority was always to impress him—with my grasp of
language, with my appreciation for adult things, with my
gifts for drawing and composition? That I seldom failed to
impress only compounded the problem.

Then, too, every boy needs the occasional paternal
"thou shalt". My moral instruction, if it could be called
that, was an open-ended dialogue with "Parviz". This
took place against the backdrop of my father's own character flaws, which with each passing year came into sharper
focus. I longed for some cosmic and moral absolutes. Yet
the only absolute command that my father handed down
to me was: "Be yourself." It was maddening. Who was this
"self" dwelling inside me, to whom I owed such fidelity?
My father wouldn't say.

CHAPTER TWO

SORROWS AND AFFLICTIONS

The children of secular, liberal people tend to grow up assuming that everyone is as secular and liberal as their parents. That was the case with me. I had some exposure to religion at home, of course. Baba Nasser and Maman Farah were believers, and every day I would catch them immersed in prayer in a corner of their bedroom that faced Mecca. I liked to sneak behind them and imitate their movements, now kneeling, now prostrating myself, now swiveling my head to the right and to the left. But this was childish play. I didn't know the Arabic words to the prayers. My elders didn't think it necessary to teach them to me.

For my grandparents, Islam was a private matter. Maman Farah would don the hijab only at prayer time. She saw the compulsory public veiling introduced by the new regime as an irritating imposition. Her brand of Islam was at peace with the occasional glass of wine. Baba Nasser may have been slightly more orthodox. But he had a passive constitution, and my parents' decidedly un-Islamic lives probably dampened any enthusiasm he might have had for transmitting his faith to his grandson.

It wasn't until I started my formal education that I realized how Islam—Shiite Islam, to be precise—permeates Iranian life. Here was an immense spiritual, legal, and normative dominion that counted me as a subject, irrespective of my personal feelings about the matter. In school,

I also discovered the Shiite faith's jagged beauty and deep pathos. Most important, I learned about Hussein ibn Ali, the third Shiite imam and the greatest martyr in a faith of martyrs. To this day, I hear in Hussein's story an echo of Christ's teaching that "greater love has no man than this, that a man lay down his life for his friends" (Jn 15:13).

* * * * *

The historian Edward Gibbon wrote: "In a distant age and climate, the tragic scene of [Hussein's] death will awaken the sympathy of the coldest reader." In spirit and climate, the Iran of my childhood was probably closer to Hussein's late-seventh-century Arabia than Gibbon's Georgian England was. You can imagine, then, how much more intense was my sympathy for Hussein once it was awakened. The agent of that awakening was my elementary school Qur'an teacher.

At an Iranian school, a Qur'an teacher wears many hats. He trains pupils to read, memorize, and recite the Muslim holy book. He also acts as a sort of resident ideologue, forming young minds to detest America and Western "cultural imperialism", to defend the nation, to obey the supreme leader without question. It helps, too, to be a good actor and storyteller, because the Shiite rituals he is called to perform are nothing if not dramatic.

My Qur'an teacher at Shahid Sadoughi Elementary was particularly adept at this last function. Mr. Sadeghi was tall and swarthy, with a thick, perennially unkempt beard and a bearing that resembled an angry gorilla's. He wore sweat-stained, ill-fitting shirts, untucked and buttoned to the collar (but sans tie). It was the uniform of the *hezbollahi*, a "partisan of God" and a true believer in the revolution. Among students he was notorious for his sadistic streak in matters disciplinary. Those who crossed him found themselves holding stress positions—lifting one leg and the next at a ninety-degree angle, among others—for twenty or thirty minutes at a time. A slap from him sent most kids reeling. Mr. Sadeghi was a bruiser.

Toward the end of the fifth grade, when we were on the cusp of graduating to middle school, he required my class to memorize several long chapters of the Qur'an, amounting to about 5 percent of the whole text, over two months. It was a final project seemingly designed to aggravate students from secular backgrounds. Children from religious families would memorize large chunks, or even the entirety, of the Qur'an at home under parental pressure or of their own volition; it came naturally to them.

I struggled badly. Watching my agony over this assignment proved too much for my mother. She organized a small group of like-minded parents, and they took their complaints to the headmaster. The parents couldn't object to the principle that young Muslims should commit Qur'anic verses to memory. But they argued that being compelled to memorize so much in such a short time would sour the boys on scripture. Incredibly, teacher and headmaster relented. In the end, we had to memorize only two or three short chapters. Thenceforth Mr. Sadeghi became much more circumspect in dealing with me.

It was a bittersweet triumph. I loathed this man. He was the very type of the uncouth provincial who, thanks to the revolution, had suddenly come to wield great authority in a big-city school. Yet I also associated him with the most pious feelings that I had as a boy in Iran. These feelings invariably centered on the passion and martyrdom of Imam Hussein.

Every year, during the Shiite mourning month of Muharram, the headmaster would summon the teachers and the student body from their classrooms to the schoolyard.

All were required to show up, even the Armenian Christians. We arranged ourselves in neat rows, the youngest at
the front and the oldest to the back. When a black-clad Mr.
Sadeghi ascended the elevated platform at the front, we
knew the show was about to begin.

His heavy breathing blared on the speakers for a few
minutes while he waited for the boys to settle down.
Then, once he had our attention, Mr. Sadeghi teleported
our minds and souls to Arabia in the year 680. The House
of Islam was divided. Having united under the banner of
Muhammad, who claimed to have brought God's final and
fullest revelation to mankind, the Arabs were divided once
more, over who should succeed the late prophet as caliph
and commander of the faithful.

"It wasn't supposed be like this," Mr. Sadeghi said.
"The prophet, peace be upon him, hadn't been dead for
fifty years. His testament was etched in living memory."
He lowered his voice almost to a whisper and repeated the
last few words: ". . . in living memory."

At this, he began rhythmically beating his chest with the
open palm of his right hand. The other teachers and we
students followed suit. The sound of some four hundred
men and boys beating their chests filled the schoolyard.

Slap! Slap! Slap!

We now stood at the origin of the Sunni-Shiite schism
that has racked the Muslim world for nearly fourteen hundred years. Sunnis accept the legitimacy of a succession of
caliphs chosen by Muslim leaders after the prophet's death.
But Shiites believe that the right of succession belonged to
the Ahl al-Bayt, the members of Muhammad's household
who descended from his cousin and son-in-law, Ali ibn
Abi Talib.

"This was a time of injustice and unbelief," our teacher
went on, his voice rising again. "Decadent men arose,

who would usurp the heritage of the prophet himself ...
the heritage of the prophet, peace be upon him."

Slap! Slap! Slap!

Mr. Sadeghi was referring to the Sunni caliph Yazid.
Having inherited the throne from his father—a dynastic
passage that Shiites saw as a breach of an earlier accord
between the two sects—Yazid set out to consolidate his
power. From his base in Damascus, he demanded *bay'ah*
(allegiance) from every Arab chieftain and Muslim figure
of consequence. Ali and his elder son, Hassan, had been
assassinated in the course of earlier strife. It fell to Ali's
second son, Hussein, to uphold the honor of the prophet's
household.

Hussein, whose lips Muhammad had kissed, wouldn't
bow to a corrupt, worldly potentate. He withheld his
bay'ah from Yazid and soon was threatened at his home in
Medina. He took refuge briefly in Mecca before decamp-
ing for Kufa, in Iraq. Word had come to Hussein that
some 140,000 Muslims in Kufa were prepared to back him
against Yazidian despotism. Hussein agreed to take command of the insurgency, though his divine foreknowledge
told him that the cause was doomed.

Mr. Sadeghi, his voice now breaking with sobs, recalled
Hussein's words: "These people will search me out and
put me to death in Mecca and Medina, and I do not wish
the sanctity of Mecca and Medina to be violated by the
shedding of my blood." Our teacher added: "Oh Hussein,
would that we could be with you now, following your
blessed footsteps on that desert road. Oh, that we could
shield your precious body and blood from the swords and
arrows of the enemy!"

Slap! Slap! Slap!

No welcome party from Kufa greeted Hussein when
he crossed the Arabian Peninsula into Iraq. Unbeknownst

to Hussein, the city's governor had already crushed the uprising in Kufa, killing some of the rebels and buying off others. Hussein's "army" consisted of seventy-two loyal companions, plus an entourage of thirsty and famished women and children.

The sun blazed mercilessly in the sky above Mesopotamia as Hussein's scouts scanned the horizon. What at first appeared to Hussein's party like palm trees gleaming in the distance turned out to be a force of more than thirty thousand troops, including five thousand on horseback. Yazid's army had cut off Hussein from the waters of the Euphrates and blocked the way to Kufa. The trap was set. Hussein and his companions pitched camp at a place called Karbala, on the banks of the river.

"Karbala", according to the Shiites, means "the land of sorrows and afflictions".

"On the night before Ashura, that is, the tenth day of Muharram," said Mr. Sadeghi, his voice descending to a whisper once more, "Hussein gathered his companions and told them, 'I have released your *bay'ah*. Anyone who wishes to take leave unharmed, let him use the cover of darkness to flee. You would not dishonor yourself if you choose to abandon me.' "

Not one of the seventy-two took him up on the face-saving offer. "When we are right," said one, "what fear do we have of death, which would bring us to the prophet?" Come morning, Hussein and his friends and family members would enter the house of death—and then paradise.

Slap! Slap! Slap!

* * * * *

Beginning in elementary school, I was made to understand that Hussein's sacrifice at Karbala was about more than a right of succession. Karbala was ultimately about resisting the triumph of the lie. Yazid, the enemy, ruled a nascent Muslim empire, yet he lived a debauched life. Claiming the title of commander of the faithful, he laid siege against the grandson of the prophet. His troops starved children and rained arrows on holy men and women. Yazid was the perpetual hypocrite, and in every age right down to our own, upright people had to face him in the perpetual Karbala. As I grew older, it dawned on me that I lived in a Yazidian world, though it claimed the banner of Hussein and Karbala.

* * * * *

In 1991, when I was six, my parents filed for divorce. It was a mutual decision, and the process itself was relatively painless. There was only one wrinkle: me.

Parviz and Niloofar wanted to insulate me from the reality that ours was a broken family. Instead of telling me the truth about their divorce, they played what amounted to a very elaborate, adult version of the children's game house—for seven years. Other players included my grandparents, my parents' friends, and many of our relatives. They all knew about the legal state of the marriage, but for my sake they helped maintain the charade. For seven years, I assumed that my parents were in a normal, if at times rocky, marriage.

I should have been suspicious. Shortly after the divorce, my uncle in Utah filed papers to bring my mother and me to America under the family-preference visa program. This I was informed about. It might take years, I gathered, but a document called a *green kart* would eventually open the gates to my promised land.

Yet there was no talk of my father joining us in America. I knew that he couldn't travel abroad for reasons of his own making. From time to time, he would tell me of the

marvels and wonders I would see in America. Parviz didn't
include himself in these American reveries. He never said
"we" would do this or that in the United States, only
"you". I think he was readying me for the day we would
say good-bye and never see each other again. I made peace
with the prospect and lived those seven years ever aware
that a permanent separation from my father was coming.
And that was fine with me. America was home, Iran a
transitory vale.

Meanwhile, there were more immediate signs that all
was not well in the Ahmari household. My father spent
only three or four nights a week at home, sometimes
fewer. When he was with us, my parents generally kept
apart. My mother would sleep in the master bedroom,
while my father crashed on a couch in one of the spare
rooms, with the television flickering silently through the
night. Sometimes, he would spend the entire night in
front of our Amiga 600 computer, playing a rudimentary
three-dimensional game similar to Tetris. He claimed
that these smoky, sleepless nights helped him refresh his
architect's mind.

There were moments of real tenderness between my
parents and furious shouting matches in these years of
playing house. One minute, the three of us would hud-
dle and exchange kisses, and the next minute the active
volcano of marital hostility would erupt and bury all that
sweetness under lava and hot ashes. After these eruptions
ceased, each of them would seek me out separately to offer
competing accounts of the dispute. Each tried to keep me
onside, as if I were a judge or marriage counselor.

In the end, my mother won this war for my heart and
mind. She wasn't necessarily the more persuasive of the
two, but I could see plainly that Parviz Ahmari was a thoroughly irresponsible "husband" and father.

Take the matter of finances. In theory, my father was a successful architect with a comfortable income. He and his closest university friend had opened a practice together amid the building boom that followed the Iran-Iraq War. They made a good pair. His partner, Hadi, was eminently practical, and he kept my father from floating too high on the clouds of avant-garde architecture theory. The two had a natural division of labor, with my father doing more of the design and creative work and Hadi handling the business side.

My father's draft avoidance barred him from formally joining the firm as a partner. He and Hadi maintained a years-long business relationship based on trust alone. My mother was in the dark regarding these arrangements. From time to time, my father would hand her a folder stuffed with wads of cash. But there was no regularity to these payments, which I suppose amounted to a form of alimony and child support. Sometimes he would go months without paying, and when the bills piled up, he would avoid the house and render himself completely inaccessible. Baba Nasser made up the difference; my mother endured.

What was Parviz doing with his earnings? Rumors of mistresses, gambling, and opium addiction swirled around him, but I was too young to grasp such talk fully and dared not contemplate the possibility. As with the state of the marriage, I was all too willing to cooperate in my own bamboozlement.

Some things were impossible to ignore. Dining out with Hadi, his wife, and a few other close friends was a regular feature of my parents' social life; I would often tag along. When the meal was over, and it was time to pay the bill, my father would wince and make a vague hand gesture to Hadi, as if to say: Please pay this and subtract it from my account. Here was a grown man, a master architect, begging for his allowance. Hadi's nouveau riche wife would register her social triumph over my mother with a knowing smirk and raised eyebrow. My mother would blush, and I would blush for her.

But my father was never less than absolutely certain that he was faultless in all things. His critics were boobs and imbeciles, trapped by backward mentalities that he, Parviz, had long ago transcended.

One night, when I was ten or eleven years old, I pressed him about these things. There was a party at Hadi's swanky, modernist apartment, and as usual, Parviz was burning the candle at both ends. He stood in the middle of a circle of men, chaffing the others and bellowing dirty jokes over the din of electronic music. In a feat of Olympic-class carousing, he chain-smoked, took 'araq (moonshine vodka), and chased the shots with beer and spoonfuls of shallot-infused yogurt in the traditional Iranian style—all in one seamless action. His voice had gone hoarse; his face flushed crimson.

After a couple of hours, he stepped away momentarily to check on me. I must have been watching one of those Ronald Reagan–era action cartoons—*Rambo* or *G.I. Joe* or some such—on Hadi's VCR. My mood was sour. Earlier that night, I had overheard some of the women gossiping about my parents. Their tone hadn't been so much condemnatory as haughtily amused. As was often the case in these situations, I mostly felt bad for my mother. I sensed her humiliation among the wives, even if I couldn't quite articulate what it involved.

"Why do you smoke so much, Parviz?" I asked my father.

I don't know why I picked on his smoking. It was one of his many habits that attracted social derision. All of the adults in that group smoked, but none of them smoked the way my father did, burning through pack after pack, lighting his next cigarette with the last. The disapprobation that his excesses aroused, I thought, rubbed off on my mother and me.

"I know you don't like it," he replied. "I'm quit. Well, I'm *quit-ting*. Later, later."

"I think these people were talking about you and Niloofar."

"And?"

"Not in a good way."

"Let me tell you something: Ignore it. You know what they tell me? They say, 'Parviz, you're honor-less.' Fine. I don't believe this hogwash about 'honor', OK? Let them say Parviz Ahmari is honor-less."

Bighayrat, Persian for "without honor", is one of the worst things one can say about an Iranian man. It describes the kind of fellow who, in the face of an insult to his mother or sister, would slink away rather than avenge himself in a transport of rage (as Iranian society would expect him to do). My father applied the term to himself in front of me, his son.

What was I to make of this? I can't say that I was shocked, for I knew that my father wasn't like other fathers. I admired him, in the natural way that sons admire their fathers. Cracks had appeared in my picture of him, to be sure, and these were growing wider by the day. Still, this latest admission didn't obviously count against him. I had to admit: His complete disregard for the opinions of others was captivating.

In his own crapulous way, my father planted in my mind the seeds of a dangerous idea—namely, that I could, and maybe should, question the things held sacred or untouchable by others. Even honor was fair game.

* * * * *

There were hypocrisies bigger and more pernicious than my parents' sham marriage. When I was a child, the Old

Colonel's way—professing one set of values in public
while living another behind closed doors—merely struck
me as odd. But once I entered middle school and felt the
first stirrings of puberty, I found it intolerable. How so
many people maintained this duality, this studied separation of the realms, was a mystery. Worse, I had to play
along. How was I to reconcile my parents' constant exhortation to "be yourself" with Iranian reality?

The contrast between the realms appeared starker with
each passing year.

In an effort to keep the embers of their own youth
aflame, Parviz and Niloofar befriended a younger cohort
of intellectuals toward the end of the playing-house period.
Among these was a twenty-something poet named Golnar, who became something of a fixture in our house. She
was the latest in a long line of female friends whom my
mother would adopt almost as sisters. For her part, Golnar, who hailed from a traditional Kurdish family, found
among my parents' milieu a degree of personal freedom
that was unthinkable under her father's roof.

In our house, she could peruse towering shelves stacked
with Persian and Western novels as well as fine, uncensored art books. We had 'araq. We had a reliable "movie
guy", an Armenian, who, at great personal risk and meager
profits, circulated VHS copies of the latest Hollywood and
European art-house productions among families like ours.
And we had a satellite dish beaming the latest MTV music
videos and episodes of *Baywatch* and *The Simpsons* into our
living room.

Golnar, our new part-time houseguest, produced strange
and unexpected effects in me. She had a slim, shapely figure, and though her sad, Sylvia Plath airs blunted it somewhat, her intense femininity radiated powerfully all the
same. Once, I caught glimpse of her in the early morning
hours as she tiptoed to the bathroom wearing nothing but

panties and a thin white T-shirt. Thenceforth, "Golnar"—
which is to say, my fervid mental images of her—became
the primary muse to my nascent sexuality. This I reciprocated by treating the real Golnar shabbily, mocking her
poetry and various art projects.

In this department, as in others, my parents took a
hands-off approach. Rather than give me some version
of "the talk", my father bought me an educational CD-
ROM called *Understanding the Body*. It could have been
worse, I suppose. My main takeaway from the CD was
that any sexual activity could result in my immediately
dying of full-blown AIDS. Meanwhile, a classmate—by
then I was attending middle school—passed me a diskette
filled with pixelated, barely legible 1980s soft-core por-
nography. I met no parental resistance when I selected one
of the images as our computer-desktop background.

"He's just experimenting, like we used to experiment"
was a common refrain in our home.

This period of erotic bloom coincided with my first
real experience of guilt. This was no longer childish guilt,
which usually is little more than fear of punishment for bad
acts, but a worrying apprehension that I had disturbed the
proper order of things. There were no immediate, tangible
consequences when I engaged in self-abuse, whether with
Golnar on my mind or pixelated soft-core porn on my
monitor; like most boys, I learned how to evade detection.
Yet I felt bad afterward, and invariably vowed to myself
never to do it again.

A cycle of sorts was thus set in motion within me. It
began with a transgression and the guilt that it produced.
Then came those solemn resolutions to do better, which I
upheld—just until the next transgression renewed the cycle.

The nature of my bad acts also shifted around this time.
Hitherto, they had mostly aimed at ends that in themselves
weren't bad: Having lost an expensive pen that my mother

had purchased for me, for example, I might have stolen money from her to replace the gift. But now the *idea* of transgression, of being bad, became the main attraction.

* * * * *

One episode, which disquiets my conscience all these years later, took place toward the beginning of sixth grade (that is, the first year of middle school).

Each of the three grade levels at Hessam Middle School was divided into three cohorts (thus, 6-A, 6-B, 6-C, 7-A, and so on). Every few weeks, a big fight would break out between these various cohorts. One boy would shove a classmate in line for snacks. The aggrieved boy called for backup from his own cohort, and the offender did the same. Punches and kicks were exchanged, and the whole yard descended into generalized mayhem.

It was almost always the same dozen or so boys who initiated the battles, who landed the memorable punches, and who took the bulk of the punishment after the adults restored peace. They were the stars, so to speak, while the rest of us were supporting actors and extras. I would have gladly accepted the punishment—a beating from one of the assistant principals—if only I could take a star turn for once. Alas, for all my imagined bravado, I had a reputation as one of the nerdier students, and the real toughs didn't consider it worthwhile to mix it up with me.

So it was that, on this particular day, I once more found myself on the sidelines of a major melee, determined to get in on the action. I scanned the yard and spotted a pile-up in one corner. It was difficult to tell how many boys were caught in that tangle of limbs in angry motion. The target that suggested itself to me was a boy from my own cohort, who was struggling to get up from the ground as two or three others wrestled atop him. The boy's conically shaped head stuck out from under the pile.

Here was my chance to do *something*. But what? I hesitated for a second before kicking that funny-looking head of his with every ounce of strength that I could muster. The boy cried out in pain. The rest was an adrenaline-tinged blur. I was pulled into the tangle. I was punched and kicked, and I reciprocated in kind. It was invigorating. But it didn't last long. A principal's whistle rang out, and we stopped going at it. The adults rounded up the usual suspects—I wasn't one of them—and marched the rest of us to the next class, calligraphy for me.

Reason returned to me once I settled in at my desk. What had I done? Scuffling at school was bad enough. But kicking a defenseless combatant while he was down multiplied the severity of the offense. Worse, the boy belonged to my own group, and he was sitting *right there*, across the room. He was the kind of quiet, friendless boy whom other students barely noticed. Now an instant's folly had tied his fate to mine: Was he going to be all right? Did he know that it was I who had kicked him? Did anyone else see me throw the kick?

He seemed to be doing OK. There he was, sheepishly copying the lines on the blackboard into his notebook like everyone else. "You're overthinking things," I reassured myself. "He's fine." Then, halfway through class, the boy with the conical head raised his hand and asked to see the school nurse. He was bleeding from the nose.

"Oh God," I said to myself. "His brains are melting right out! His mind is going to stop working any minute now. He'll collapse and die. You'll be tried. Convicted. Executed in public. You'll be made an example for other cowardly boys across the land." My heart raced, and I could feel it pounding in the back of my throat.

Ten minutes later, the boy came back, a bloody napkin stuffed into his nose, and resumed his work. He really was going to be fine. Maybe his nosebleed wasn't even related

to my kick. Still, I had to be sure. Before the final bell
sounded, I sidled up to him more than once, offering oily
words of concern. His cogent answers demonstrated that
his brain was working, and the fact that he didn't immediately jump me further confirmed that he didn't suspect
me. I really had gotten away with it.

Yet I couldn't let the incident go. I lost my appetite in
the days that followed. I could barely sleep, and when I
did, I had nightmares. My usual comic books and cartoons
held no interest for me. My mind, it seemed, was punish-
ing me for an act that the real world of consequences had,
for all intents and purposes, forgiven.

Finally, I fessed up to my mother about what had happened. For once, she lost her temper. Her first step was
to confiscate all of my contraband VHS copies of *G.I. Joe*,
Transformers, *WrestleMania*, and the like. Anxiety about
the psychological effects of violent media on children had
spread to Iran by then, and my mother was convinced
that I had acted out under the influence of these tapes;
she would return them to me a week or so later. Next, she
resolved that we would march to the other boy's house,
where I was to apologize to him and his parents.

My victim's home was only a few blocks from our
house, yet a cultural and material chasm separated our two
families. Hitherto, I had visited the homes of boyhood
friends only from my own social milieu. Here, then, was
my first real encounter with poverty in Iran and the mystery of human fortune.

The woman who greeted us at the entrance, the boy's
mother, was dressed in a full veil that covered all but her
eyes and nose. My mother briefly explained the purpose
of our visit. The other invited us in. She was gracious. We
followed her up a darkened stairwell to reach an apartment
on the third floor. Standing inside the door was my classmate, and peeking out from behind him was a younger

boy, presumably his little brother. There was no sign of a father. Was he imprisoned or martyred in the war? I never found out. The mother ushered us in.

Their apartment was tiny—only slightly larger than the room that I had to myself—and utterly barren. The family had no books or records. There were no paintings or sculptures or other art objects, save for a framed piece of calligraphy that was hanging in one corner, above an old television with a wooden box. A garlicky smell wafted in from the kitchen, mixing with the rosewater scent of the living area to create an evil, eye-watering effect.

Our hostess removed her veil but not the floral head-scarf she wore underneath. "Please, have a seat," she said, before scurrying to the kitchen to brew tea.

There were no seats. The pillows and blankets that were rolled up next to the walls served as bedding at night and apparently doubled as furniture during the day. "Please, I know our house isn't worthy of you," the woman added.

In one swift motion my mother plopped herself cross-legged and pulled me down next to her. The two boys wouldn't sit until their mother emerged from the kitchen to serve hot tea from a plastic tray. With the requirements of traditional hospitality out of the way, she sat down across from my mother; only then did her children join her on the floor, one flanking her on each side.

"So," she said, "how may we be of service to you?"

My mother jabbed me with an elbow, as if to say: Spill it out! An excruciating interval passed, but I couldn't find the words. My mother took it upon herself to detail what had happened, only leaving a blank spot for me to fill in at the end: "... and Sohrab wishes to express his ..."

"I'm so, so sorry!" I blurted, and fell silent once more.

Our hostess considered what had been said for a minute. Then she replied: "You needn't have come here. Boys get into brawls all the time. My boy was fighting, too.

Anyway, he always tells me how much he admires your
Mr. Sohrab. You folks needn't apologize to us."

I wished I could have melted into the floor, for shame. I
couldn't bear to look at my classmate and his mother. My
eyes darted around the room, seeking something else to see.
They came to rest on the calligraphy hanging on the wall.
There, inscribed for praise and protection, was the name of
God: ALLAH. Instantly, I recalled Hussein and Karbala. My
old Qur'an teacher's voice resounded in my mind:

> Oh Hussein, would that we could be with you now,
> on that desert road to Kufa. Oh Hussein, your children
> rubbed empty waterskins on their little bellies, but it
> offered them no relief from the thirst and the heat. You
> rode gallantly to the enemy line and held up your fam-
> ished infant, hoping that the hypocrites might be moved
> to mercy. But, oh Hussein, they shot an arrow through
> the babe's throat. Hussein, your enemies, who didn't dare
> face you from the front, ambushed you from the rear.

I pictured Hussein bent over atop his steed and clinging
tight to the lifeless infant in his arms. The horse, Zuljanah,
reared by the prophet himself, must have sensed that its master was breathing his last. A hundred arrows that had made
their mark protruded from the imam's torso and limbs. The
blood drained from his body and painted Zuljanah's shim-
mering white coat crimson. Hussein's serene visage, bathed
in divine light (as the popular portraits had it), was a judgment against me. What a hypocrite I had been, what a sniv-
eling little Yazid. I was overcome with pity for my classmate
and his family and their wretched hovel, for that warrior-
imam of seventh-century Arabia and his sacrifice.

But did I believe in Hussein's God? Yes, but I wouldn't
for much longer.

Chapter Three

Of God and *Djinn*

If "God is love" (1 Jn 4:8), it follows that God is also a conversation, or a dialogue, between a lover and a beloved. The author of creation invites each of us to converse with him, not from any lack or need on his part, but out of the sheer, gratuitous love that animates his creative action. We meet him, first, in that interior place of encounter called the soul. With prayerful minds and tongues and ears of faith, we address ourselves to him and are addressed in turn.

Up to a certain age, I was on friendly terms with Almighty God—this, notwithstanding my mostly secular upbringing. In the solitude that is the only child's lot, usually at night, I placed myself before him, thanked him for my blessings, and asked for more. That the subject of these praises and prayers was usually childish didn't subtract from their sincerity. But which God did I address, when I prayed that my parents might buy me that Lego set, or that I might be delivered from the dreary wages of homework? I couldn't tell you.

My family's faith, such as it was, amounted to a kind of liberal sentimental ecumenism. Islam had its worthy (read: humanistic) parts that deserved our deference. Zoroastrianism, the ancient Persian protoreligion, was revered more for patriotic than theological reasons. Christianity was simply wonderful, a gentle, Western religion, whose local adherents, the Armenians, sold us wine, *'araq*, and salami. Then there was the fortune-telling and Far East spiritualism that my mother took up, from time to time. All of these traditions and beliefs had their place. All could offer consolation at the right time. None was taken all that seriously.

Thus, on the first day of each school year, my mother or grandmother held a copy of the Qur'an so that I might kiss it on my way out the door. I kissed it gladly, and I was pretty sure that paying obeisance to the infallible and uncreated word of God would bring me success at school. When I was younger still, my mother and I would accompany my nanny to her Armenian Orthodox church. There I prayed long and passionately at the various altars. I don't remember doing so, but there is no reason to doubt my nanny's recollection. Visiting old Zoroastrian shrines and monuments in the countryside inspired similar devotion while my father discoursed on the aesthetic significance of this column and that bas-relief. Then we drove on.

And yet, as I say, the all-too-bearable lightness of my family's faith didn't stop me from speaking with God or shedding hot tears for Hussein and the other imams and martyrs. I retained my spiritual faculty and natural longing for God—that is, until I approached pubescence. Then one day, when I was twelve years old or perhaps thirteen, I stopped speaking with God. I walked away from the conversation, and more than that: I concluded that there was no one on the other end.

* * * * *

The year must have been 1997. We were vacationing in northern Iran, on the shores of the Caspian Sea, where denizens of Tehran have long found respite from the ceaseless bustle of the capital. My parents didn't own a villa by the Caspian. But they had many friends who did, and the annual "villa trip" was something of a family tradition. I trace some of my happiest memories to these trips, not least because there were usually other children around.

We would ride north in a caravan of three or four vehicles. Setting out before dawn, we would climb the hills and mountains that surround Tehran. The narrow, snaking roads were notoriously accident-prone, and for much of the journey the landscape was distinguished mainly by its desolation. At some point, however, barren soil and harsh rock formations gave way to lush, rolling hills and valleys, and the air took on a moist, velvety quality. Then came the flatlands and rice paddies. A little farther, and the waters of the Caspian came into view. We had arrived.

The days were invariably spent on the beach. Shariah law demanded strict separation of the sexes, even at sea. At most public beaches, the authorities curtained off the water to create separate men's and women's areas. Everywhere there were banners that read: "My Sister, Mind Your Veil. My Brother, Mind Your Eyes." But my parents and their friends usually discovered hidden corners where men and women could share the beach. They would even bring *'araq* hidden in plastic jars and hot-water bottles.

If members of the morality police, known as the *komiteh* (committee), showed up in their signature green Toyota 4x4s, all wasn't lost. Most of them could be bribed to overlook such iniquities as drinking alcohol and cavorting in mixed company. There was always a chance, however, that the officer in charge was a true believer. Then a flogging or even jail time could be in order. A colleague of my father's had been caught once with *'araq*—or maybe it was cassettes of Western music—in his car. Unfortunately for him, this was in the early revolutionary days, when no amount of bribery and haggling could get offenders out of punishment. The *komiteh* ordered him to be flogged; the scarring left the skin on his back looking permanently like challah bread.

Such frightful episodes—every family had at least one, and usually several—didn't make secular Iranians any less inclined to drink alcohol, gather in mixed company, or listen to Western music. Rather, the fear of getting caught only added an element of adventure to every social outing. The risk was half the fun.

That summer in question, my parents and I rode with a friend of theirs named Manuchehr, a wealthy businessman, whose own wife took a different car. There was nothing untoward in this switcheroo. My parents wished to stay with me, and Manuchehr's wife was keen to catch up with other friends, so she rode in their car. Roughly midway, we ran into a morality checkpoint. The alcohol and playing cards weren't in our vehicle, so we expected to be waved through. But the young officers found the arrangement suspicious. What was the relation between the adults in the vehicle? Were they, perhaps, lovers in a ménage à trois? And whose child was this boy? We were ordered out of the car and interrogated, first in groups, then individually.

"Does the number one-five-five-six-six-zero mean anything to you, son?" one of the officers asked me at one point.

I blanked.

"Interesting. That's supposedly your dad's identity number, but you don't know it. Veeeery interesting."

I prayed that we might be spared unpleasantness. Finally, after about two hours, it was established that Manuchehr and my mother were not lovers, that my parents had once been married, and, therefore, that I wasn't illegitimate. We were allowed to go, and made it to the villa. Our nerves were rankled, but we had a fresh war story with which to regale our travel companions.

A few days later, we had a second run-in with the *komiteh*. This time it was one of the roaming 4x4s that intruded on our sun-soaked beach idyll. Two uniformed officers and one plainclothes agent stepped out of the sport-utility vehicle. By the way the plainclothes man carried himself, it was obvious that he was the one in charge. It didn't take him long to demand the plastic hot-water bottle we had sitting on a picnic blanket. One sniff, and he knew.

"This is alcohol," he said, screwing up his face.

The men in our group were expected to respond, but what could they say? "My brother," Hadi, my father's business partner, said after a time. "We're just ... we're just having a little—"

"Shut your mouth! It's almost time for the midday prayers, and your breath smells like a whorehouse. Aren't you ashamed of yourselves, drinking in front of these children?" Here the agent turned to me. The frown lifted from his brows and something resembling a smile crossed his lips. "How old are you, my dear boy?"

"M-m-me? I'm five."

I was a few months short of thirteen. I had a teenager's body and pimples, and my voice had started to crack. What made me tell such a fantastic lie about my age? I reasoned that the officers would take it easier on us if they thought that I was much younger than I was. It worked, though for different reasons than I had supposed. Everyone, the *komiteh* men included, cracked up at the idea that I was a five-year-old. The two uniformed officers struggled to suppress their chuckles; their superior was only slightly more circumspect. The whole scene took on a surreal aspect. There was more questioning and scolding still in store for the adults, but eventually the officer in charge said: "Well, it does look like you're having fun. Why not give us a taste of your candy?"

He needn't have said more. The men quickly pooled their cash and handed all they had to the *komiteh*. The guardians of the nation's virtues went on their way.

* * * * *

The two back-to-back encounters with the regime had gone as well as anyone could have hoped. But I had had enough. That night, I retired to my room upstairs as soon as we returned to the villa. Evenings were reserved for cards and a barbecue, but I didn't feel like playing cards or horseplaying with the other kids. Maybe I had had some dispute with the adults, though I can't recall the substance.

In bed, I cursed everything. I cursed my father for being so capricious and eccentric, and my mother for being so weak. I cursed the Janus-faced Islamic Republic, at once severe and venal, pious and petty. And I cursed God. I cursed the God whose main business was apparently to interfere with people having fun on the beach, the God who required a police state to enforce his whims and whose agents were willing to cut moral corners for the right price.

One doesn't curse a nonexistent person. Cursing presumes the existence of the person (or thing) that is being cursed. But my cursing of God that night was one short step removed from atheism. Cursing him was a way to test the waters of unbelief.

* * * * *

A few years earlier, my mother had taken a job as an editorial assistant to a female novelist. The job augmented the family income and helped my mother gain entrée to the higher circles of Iranian arts and letters. She would often take me along to the novelist's grand, gloomy apartment, and there I was entrusted to the care of the live-in maid while my mother was busy in the study. The maid was a homely, illiterate old woman who loved to tell me stories about ghosts, demons, and malevolent *djinn* (supernatural beings that feature in the Qur'an).

These tales of the macabre scared me witless for years. Her various plotlines and characters are now lost to my memory. But all of her stories had the same "moral"— namely, that the evil spirits reserve the worst treatment for those mortals who dared deny their existence. It was always the skeptical characters whom the *djinn* would drag, kicking and screaming, into the netherworld, never to be seen or heard from again. There was a crude but effective mechanism against rational inquiry built into her tales. To question their veracity was to invite the wrath of the bogies.

For years afterward, whenever I found myself alone in a long, empty corridor, I would intone the words: "I believe in you, oh *djinn*. I believe that you exist." I had to keep the mantra on my tongue when navigating unfamiliar and spooky places, much as I had learned to look both ways before crossing a busy street. Yet there was a temptation— lurking at a subconscious level, because I didn't dare bring it to the forefront of my mind—to deny the existence of the *djinn*. I resisted it for as long as I could, until the headstrong boy in me got the better of my superstitious nature. Once, while I was alone in some strange house somewhere, I whispered: "I *don't* believe in you, oh *djinn*!"

I shut my eyes and prepared for the worst. But nothing happened. No spirits assailed me. After a few more tries, my fear of *djinn* dissipated altogether.

I think a similar psychological process was at work when I hurled curses at God that night in the villa. I knew that, in the order of supernatural beings, God stood higher—infinitely higher—than the average *djinn*. The price would thus be higher—infinitely higher—if I turned out to be wrong about his nonexistence. This was the same God, after all, whose intervention I had sought a couple of days earlier, while the morality committee was grilling me about my parents. But wasn't that prayer—wasn't all prayer—merely a more respectable version of the "I believe in you, oh *djinn*" mantra? What about the kissing of the Qur'an on the way out the door? Or the kneeling before the altars at my nanny's church? Or the beating of the chest in sorrow and reverence for the Shiite martyrs?

Didn't I perform these acts of devotion to put my mind at ease in the face of the unknown? If the *djinn* didn't attack me, was it because the mantra "worked", or because there was no such thing as *djinn*? If the school year was successful, if my parents bought me that Lego set, if the morality police didn't flog my loved ones—was it prayer that "worked"? Or would the same results have obtained had I *not* prayed in those instances? What if I cursed God? Or denied his existence?

"Let's give it a try," I said to myself. "To hell with God! Damned be God!"

Nothing happened. "How about this? There is no God!"

Nothing. What rank nonsense, this God business. Right then and there, I became an atheist.

There was more to it than that, of course. Living in an Islamic theocracy—where God appears in the form of floggings and judicial amputations, scowling ayatollahs and secret police—has a way of souring one on things divine. Years later, I read a wise young Iranian dissident, who argued that if the Islamic Republic collapsed one day, it would leave behind the world's largest community of atheists. This is a perfectly plausible theory.

My turn away from God had something to do as well with the nature of the Islam of Khomeini and his followers, a religion that *never* proposes but only *imposes*—and that by the sword or the suicide bomber.

There is good and beauty in Islam, to be sure (the sacrifice of Hussein at Karbala most readily comes to mind). But in broad swaths of the Islamic world, the religion of Muhammad is synonymous with law and political dominion without love or mercy. Islam is, as the French philosopher Pierre Manent has written, a "starkly objective" faith. Where it spreads, a set of authoritative norms and a political community follow. To assent to the law and the community is to assent to Islam. There is little room for the individual conscience and free will, for the human heart, for reason and intellect.

And what was I then but an aspiring intellectual? Already at age twelve, I wanted to join the creative class—the painters, poets, literary critics, and novelists among whom I was growing up. This aspiration was closely bound up with a certain image of Western-style secularity.

The ideal type of the Iranian intellectual was a ponytailed, mustachioed man in his forties or fifties. He would be pictured on the dust jacket of his monograph on Baudelaire, looking pensive while holding a lit cigarette against his right temple. Before I had a single worthwhile idea of my own, and while still playing with action figures, I knew that *that* was who I was destined to be. And what did this fellow think about God and religion? After the revolution, he feigned a degree of piety in public, of course, to keep his head. But chances were, he was a nonbeliever at heart. He may have permitted, at most, a sort of poetic spiritualism. But he abhorred religion, which he associated with backwardness and provincialism. I knew this, because I had met dozens of members of the species. Atheism, then, was also a prerequisite of my future vocation.

Finally, hadn't my father urged me to be myself, to cut my own path across life's thicket of choices? Well, I would do just that. It didn't occur to me at the time that, in the name of independence and originality, I was, in fact, adopting someone else's persona, a prefabricated cultural type.

As for my soul, that night's curses and declaration of unbelief caused no immediately discernible effects. It would take me years, decades even, to notice that I had been dragged—that I had dragged myself—into a nether-world of a kind. No cartoonish demons inhabited it, but there *were* demons, and it *was* a netherworld all the same.

* * * * *

By my own dim lights, I had hit upon a potent and forbid-den idea that was reserved for only the most daring think-ers. I was on constant lookout for openings into which I might inject my transgressive new notions. Yet I was prudent enough not to proclaim my unbelief everywhere. At home, I told everyone but stopped short of telling Baba Nasser that I was an unbeliever—not because I feared his reaction but because I didn't want to agitate the old man's soul. But I did assail other things he held dear: Islam and Iranian nationalism and our republic.

"Aren't we backward, Baba?" I would ask him. "Shouldn't our women be free to wear what they want in public?" And before he could properly respond, I would pepper him with more questions and retorts until he became flustered and bid me to leave him be.

I also extended my great rebellion to middle school but, again, without declaring outright that I was an atheist. Doing so, I knew, could have gotten my parents and me into big trouble. But I incessantly praised the West and even the United States, our archenemy, as a way of spiting my teachers. I copied out a children's encyclopedia entry on ancient Rome, for example, and recited it before my English class in a striking American accent. Or in art class, I would draw characters from *G.I. Joe* and make a point of emphasizing the American flags emblazoned on their combat gear. These were coded assaults on the regime's Islamist values, and they were received as such.

My primary antagonist in middle school was, once again, my Qur'an teacher. His name was Mr. Pourmand, and he was far more sophisticated than the knuckle-dragging Mr. Sadeghi from elementary. Though he dressed like a *hezbollahi*, Mr. Pourmand was clean-cut and even dashing. He never beat the students, moreover, using charm and reasoned words instead to win them to his side. He was always available after school for counseling or to play soccer. He was popular.

Mr. Pourmand must have figured early on that I would be trouble, and he had a plan. Instead of confronting my pro-Western outbursts head-on, he would take them in stride, as if he couldn't care less what I thought about Islam or the regime. He would use my own vanity to bring me down, judo style. Thus, rather than lecture me about hewing to the righteous path and so forth, he offered me the chance to be celebrated for my talents.

In the seventh grade, he cast me in one of the lead roles in a play he had written about the 1987 massacre of Shiite pilgrims to Mecca at the hands of Saudi security forces. I decided that it was worth it to mouth his stilted, hackneyed dialogue—the theme was Sunni villainy and Shiite victimhood—if it meant stage stardom. The same year, he put my knack for illustration to use by having me paint a U.S. flag—so that it could be burned in an anti-American demonstration he was organizing at school. I appreciated his tawdry attentions and so went along each time.

In the end, though, the transactional nature of our rapport meant that he didn't get very far with me. I would cooperate with his various projects only insofar as they won me recognition, but I held on to my adolescent certainties for the most part. Thus, he would encourage me to read good Islamic texts and reflect on them during the holidays, and I would return raving about Jules Verne and Mark Twain. His frustration showed.

"See, that's just the kind of decadent garbage you Westoxicated types would read," he said, tongue only partially in cheek. "Westoxication", or "Weststruckness", was an Islamist slur for secular Iranian intellectuals, who, lacking confidence in their own culture and identity, pathetically aped Western ways and ideas.

Then, too, I gradually caught on that Mr. Pourmand wasn't all that confident in his own certainties. I caught a glimmer of interest in his eyes when I told him that my family had a "great" movie guy and that we usually got to watch the latest releases not long after they debuted in America and Europe. He muttered something in disapproval at first and left it at that. Then, a few days later, he asked me to stay after Qur'an class. He had a favor to ask. "Could your parents, um, let me borrow, um, some of your tapes?" He was especially eager to watch *Titanic*. My mother obliged.

* * * * *

News of our imminent departure from Iran put the final nail in Mr. Pourmand's efforts to correct my ideological disorders. In the fall of 1998, when I was thirteen, the U.S. State Department invited my mother and me for an interview. The mythical *green kart* would soon be ours. The

1979 revolution and hostage crisis had severed diplomatic ties between Washington and Tehran. So we had to travel to Ankara for U.S. consular services.

My mother, Baba Nasser, and I boarded the next available bus to the Turkish capital. Several heart-stopping moments marked this road trip, the most decisive and life-altering I ever took. The first came at the Iranian side of the border, where the guards held our bus for nearly an hour while they observed the passengers from a nearby garrison. The claustrophobia and feeling of being watched by unseen figures filled us with dread, one of our government's specialties.

After the hour passed, a couple of guards boarded the bus and selected a few passengers, seemingly at random, for interviews and luggage searches. We weren't chosen. Then the bus was allowed to proceed. Relief came when we saw Kemal Mustafa Atatürk, the founder of the modern Turkish republic, whose stern, resolute visage stared down at us from a portrait hanging at the passport control on the other side.

Turkey's political and administrative center, Ankara lacks the architectural splendor of Istanbul. I didn't mind. What mattered was that Ankara was *khaareji* (foreign), which meant, of course, better. The supermarkets were well lit and had that synthetic scent of Western-ness that I knew and loved from my grandparents' luggage. You could even watch uncensored Hollywood movies in the theaters, a major improvement over the low-quality VHS recordings that we were used to.

I remember my mother at one point screaming on the telephone at my Uncle Farzin, who had forgotten to fax over some necessary document or other. More than once amid these frenetic moments, we despaired that the green cards would slip from our grasp. But on our third or fourth appointment at the U.S. Embassy, we were handed a pair of manila envelopes. Inside were documents that would allow us to enter America as "permanent resident aliens". The envelopes were sealed with red stamps, and it was impressed upon us that they mustn't be opened until we landed in America, and then only by immigration authorities.

I was in the eighth grade, but there was no going back to school when we returned to Tehran. We had only a few weeks to pack our bags and make final preparations before flying to our new home. I did stop by the middle school with my mother to say good-bye. When I had first told Mr. Pourmand that my family was immigrating to the United States, he had snapped back: "Of course. That's where Westoxicated fools like you belong." But on this last visit, he asked my mother's advice about the green card process. He, too, hankered for the Great Satan's embrace.

Our relatives and friends tendered their best wishes. "This regime's expiration date is almost up," the Old Colonel said to me. "So you'll go to America, you'll get educated, and you'll come back and become *somebody*, and by then Iran will be free."

Parting from my father turned out to be harder than I had imagined. I sobbed hysterically when we said our farewell. He handed me a tattered copy of J.D. Salinger's *Catcher in the Rye* in Persian translation and a Japanese Noh mask with an impish expression. I never figured out what to make of the mask. As for the novel, I didn't finish it until a couple of years after we immigrated. It would take another decade to solve the psychological puzzle: Parviz thought of himself as a Holden Caulfield of sorts. He would rage against the "phonies" all his life and preserve his wildness in bohemian amber.

"Whenever you need to reach me," he said on our last day together, "all you have to do is close your eyes, concentrate really hard, and make telepathic contact. And stay alert for my telepathic signals, too!" It was just as well that he was committed to this one, extrasensory communication channel, because he was otherwise disinclined to answer my letters and phone calls, as I would soon learn. We were out of touch for most of the two decades that followed; he died in 2017.

* * * * *

In November 1998, shortly before Thanksgiving Day, my mother, grandmother, and I boarded a KLM Royal Dutch Airlines flight from Tehran to Salt Lake City. An hour after takeoff, a flight attendant announced: "Ladies and gentlemen, we have left the airspace of the Islamic Republic of Iran." Niloofar and Maman Farah took off their headscarves. The passengers clapped, whooped, and hollered, and we joined in.

Chapter Four

Resident Alien

One of the most devious tricks that our minds play on us is to hold on to an imagined impression of a person, place, or thing long after experience proves that impression to be false. We form an opinion of someone whom we haven't met out of tidbits of information and half-correct inferences, and our imagination fills in the remaining gaps. We impose our own categories on the other and cling to our imaginary idea of him, even when he is standing before us in the flesh and telling us that we are wrong. "No, no," we insist. "My imagination must prevail."

A similar psychological process was at work when I first arrived in the United States. For all my enthusiasm for America and Americanism, I had no tangible sense of what this new country was all about. America, I thought, would be something like our own little circle of Iranian intellectuals, writ large. Every corner of it would be urban and "advanced", chic and clean. And it would be devoid of religion, because irreligion was the hallmark of freedom.

That I was immersed in American popular culture and spoke English fluently before I left Iran only compounded my misapprehensions. It would have been one thing if I needed to learn a new language and culture from scratch. That, at least, would have impelled me to open my eyes and ears to the new reality. But I could read, write, and speak English with ease, and I imagined that I had already mastered American culture: What was left to know after watching *Star Wars*, *The Silence of the Lambs*, *Dances with Wolves*, and the like? I wasn't in America to hear what it had to say to me. I was there because that was where I belonged, and because I had so much to say to and about America.

Yet reality always breaks through, and it didn't take too long to do so with me. Although America's elite culture was indeed largely secular, that culture coexisted with pockets of intense religiosity. And for all the individual liberties enshrined in the U.S. Constitution, Americans could be intensely communitarian, even conformist. This mismatch, between America as I had imagined it and as it really was, became a great source of anguish for me. I reacted by picking up my rebellion—against God, religious faith, and authority—where I had left it off in Iran.

* * * * *

Eden, Utah (population six hundred), is a tiny ski town in the Rockies, a couple of hours' drive north from Salt Lake City. My Uncle Farzin and his family lived a bucolic life in Eden, and it became our first home after we emigrated from Iran. Utah was a promised land, a Zion, for its mostly Mormon inhabitants. But it was not the promised land that I had expected.

If I were one for fishing, skiing, or horse riding, I would have found much to delight me in northern Utah. It was a place of astounding natural beauty. The snow-capped peaks of the Wasatch Range rose majestically above the verdant hills and valleys around my uncle's house. The nearby Pineview Reservoir gathered the pristine waters of the Ogden River, used to irrigate the area's patchwork of perfectly geometric farms. The air was cool and crisp, and the sky seemed somehow bigger and wider than I remembered it from the old country.

Too bad I didn't have the slightest appreciation for the outdoors (and still don't). Just as in Iran, my life in Utah revolved around books, movies, and music, most belonging to that genre of lowbrow culture that tries to pass itself off as something slightly higher and therefore appeals to adolescents who think they are endowed with excellent taste.

Think, for example, of *The X-Files*, the *Alien* franchise, and the like, which I could now watch on American television. The slimy, slithering, hyperintelligent monsters from outer space were part of the appeal, of course. But it seemed to me that the aliens were mere props in the more fascinating human drama of these movies and television shows. The real villains were the governments or corporations that hid the truth from humanity or sought to exploit the aliens for their own nefarious ends.

In Iran, this cynical aspect of American science fiction had eluded my understanding. But once I got to Utah, the conspiratorial sci-fi plot took on a fresh resonance, as I redirected my oppositional energies away from the mullahs and toward America's faceless corporate bureaucrats. I mistook sci-fi schlock for penetrating social critique, and the genre's paranoid currents began to shape my view of the new country.

Or take the music of Pink Floyd, with its psychedelic roots, operatic pretentions, and trite lyrics. I had fallen in love with Floyd in Iran, but now I could purchase original, shrink-wrapped CDs in the stores. For my first Christmas, my uncle and his wife bought me a copy of the band's 1979 double album, *The Wall*, which chronicles a rock star's mental breakdown. I would blast *The Wall* in my little room in Uncle Farzin's house, air drumming or strumming on an imaginary guitar while joining my voice to lyricist Roger Waters': "We don't need no ed-yu-caytion! We don't need no thought controwwwl!"

Those lyrics notwithstanding, I was elated when my mother enrolled me at the local middle school in Eden. There I finished the ninth grade before we moved to a different town, Logan, so she could study for a master's degree in fine arts at the local university while I attended high school. Here was my chance to shine among my rightful peers—those freethinking young Americans, who, I was certain, all reverenced Pink Floyd, detested religiosity, and thrilled to tales of extraterrestrial visitors and conspiratorial G-men in black suits.

I was unpleasantly surprised to learn that, in fact, high school life in Utah gravitated toward athletics (football, especially), dances and dating, and Mormonism—none of which interested me and some of which positively repulsed me.

Start with the athletics. Every few weeks, we were ushered out of class into a big assembly to cheer our teams ahead of basketball and football matches. Not having the slightest talent or inclination for sports, I found the pep rally to be a source of puzzlement. Why were we asked to identify with this animal mascot, the Grizzly? How could an animal embody our "school spirit"? What was school spirit anyway? To be sure, the sight of the cheerleaders, with their short glittering dresses and long American legs, was an improvement over the lachrymose, all-male assemblies for Imam Hussein. Still, I couldn't bring myself to even feign excitement about a ball game between two sets of teenagers from nearby small towns. Surrounded by hundreds of cheering boys and girls, I felt utterly alone.

My alienation wasn't limited to school. Social life in Utah, such as it was, never rose above sports talk and small talk. Our Utahan friends—including my uncle's American in-laws and a set of thoroughly Americanized Iranians—could spend hours talking about absolutely nothing that mattered (to me). If it wasn't the latest Utah Jazz or Denver Broncos game, then the company would be absorbed in talk about the weather and road conditions.

"Can you believe it, this jerk in a Ram tailed me through the whole canyon with his brights on? I kept slowin' down. I says, I says to myself, 'Well, if you're in such a hurry, just pass me already, buddy! ... If you think this winter's bad, then you musta forgotten—what was it, dear, two years ago or three? Oh, was it three, when the snow was piled so high we couldn't open the door? ... I says to my wife, I says, 'Why don't we chop our own firewood?' So this year we started doin' that, and we're savin' *a whole lot.* How much, dear? See, we're savin' a hundred bucks a month just doin' that! 'Course, it breaks your back ...'"

When weather talk died down, the discussion would shift to new cars, classic cars, trucks, snowplows, snowblowers, tools, and the prices of these things. This wheelsand-gears babble I found so tedious as to make me long for the weather talk. For all the miseries of the Islamic Republic, there at least people had something to say. Wasn't the point of social life to discuss politics, art, and ideology? In America, my ability to parrot the elevated talk of adults was severely undervalued, because the adults themselves weren't all that into elevated things.

* * * * *

Schoolwork provided an escape from this overwhelming banality. Like many immigrant children, I figured out that schooling in the United States is less demanding, in part because it doesn't emphasize rote learning of facts and figures. Applying the same or even less effort than in the old country could yield much better results in America. I became a teacher's darling, much as I had been in Iran (the Qur'an teachers excepted). But there was more to high school than academics, and other areas besides athletics where I came up woefully short.

One of them was American vernacular. Though I knew my way around American popular culture, there were plenty of slang terms and common idioms that I didn't follow. On my first or second day at junior high, for example, one of my new classmates asked my name, and when I told him what it was, he replied: "Sohrab, huh? That's a badass name!"

I was indignant: "Bad ass? What do you mean, bad ass? Your own ass is bad!"

My pronunciation was also often shaky. This was a problem, given my proclivity for using ten-dollar words that I had read in books but never heard out loud. Thus a teacher might have asked me: "How are you feeling today, Sohrab?"

And I would have responded: "Oh, just a little *melan-cow-lick*."

Another problem was girls. To wit, being secular-minded in Iran was one thing; the free and close proximity to the opposite sex in school was something else. Even in the most liberal Iranian circles, there was always a separation between men and women, at least when they first met. At the American junior high, that invisible wall between the sexes didn't exist. This was driven home for me one morning, when a pair of fellow ninth graders—cheerleaders and "besties"—approached me in the hallway. One girl was carrying the other in her arms.

Her voice strained by mock exhaustion, the one doing the carrying yelled out: "Yoo-hoo! *So*-rab! Help me with her; she's getting too much for me!"

Both of them giggled. I froze.

"Come on, *So*-rab!" said the one being carried, as they got closer to me. More giggling.

I couldn't move. The thought of touching (holding!) a girl—and not any girl, but one of those all-American blonds, her curves offset by figure-hugging clothes and towering wedge heels—boggled my mind. Sweat poured from my body. My face burned red hot. In the end, rather than take the opportunity, I mumbled something incoherent and sped away in the opposite direction, to howls of laughter from the two girls.

Afterward, I carefully cropped my mental picture of the episode—omitting any recollection of my own sexual pusillanimity—and added it to my growing personal archive of impure thoughts for later use. The two girls were being more playful than flirtatious. Such teasing was part and parcel of teenage life in Utah, and it was mostly innocent. But in the moment, it was all too much for my fresh-off-the-boat Iranian mind.

Years later, I read about the life of Sayyid Qutb, the Egyptian educator and literary critic who was one of the founding theorists of modern Islamism. In 1949, a forty-three-year-old Qutb traveled to Greeley, Colorado, to study at a teachers college. In the book he subsequently published about his two years in Colorado, Qutb wrote of how "the American girl is well acquainted with her body's seductive capacity. She knows it lies in the face, and in expressive eyes, and thirsty lips. She knows seductiveness lies in the round breasts, the full buttocks, and in the shapely thighs, sleek legs—and she shows all this and does not hide it."

The midcentury Colorado he saw was still very much a culturally conservative place. Its sexually charged atmosphere outraged Qutb, even so. In addition to 1940s "seductresses", he recoiled at what he observed during a dance night in a church basement: "They danced to the tunes of the gramophone, and the dance floor was replete with tapping feet, enticing legs, arms wrapped around waists, lips pressed to lips, and chests pressed to chests."

Qutb's time in Greeley confirmed his hatred of the West, which he equated with *jahiliyya*—ignorance, materialism, animalistic conduct. When he went home, he signed up for the Muslim Brotherhood and spent the rest of his life calling for the overthrow of secular governments in the Arab world. Allah's laws, he taught, must regulate every sphere of life among Muslims, especially relations between the sexes. The Egyptian government executed Qutb in 1966. His writings would later inspire Osama bin Laden, and still today jihadists from the Philippines to Nigeria revere Qutb.

Like Greeley in 1949, the Utah of the 1990s was relatively conservative by American standards of the time. And like Qutb, I was nevertheless shocked by the easy sexual mores that I witnessed. My reaction, however, was radically different from the Egyptian's. His country had been governed by secular and modernizing authorities, first the Muhammad Ali dynasty and later Gamal Abdel Nasser's socialist republic; it was the latter that put him to death.

By contrast, I had left an Iran that had recently re-Islamized itself, and the re-Islamization was one major reason for my departure. Thus, faced with those two girls and numerous other episodes of the kind, the thought that "the ayatollah was right all along" never even crossed my mind. Rather, I took my discomfort at physical contact with strange women to be a shortcoming—on my part. I was insufficiently modern and rational in my habits and ways.

* * * * *

As if the awkwardness of landing fresh off the boat weren't enough, I had also to contend with a hitherto unfamiliar problem: poverty. In Tehran, you will recall, we lived in a roomy two-story house. The family coffers had taken some hits after the revolution, to be sure, not least owing to my father's erratic finances. Still, we never felt less than middle class. Once we left my Uncle Farzin's and moved to Logan, we could barely afford bargain-store groceries with coupons, and we lived in a house with wheels under it. We had become *déclassé*.

Many Iranian immigrants like to boast of how they arrived in the United States with barely twenty dollars in their pockets and went on to prosper in business, academe, or the professions. We didn't start out from such a dire place, but we were financially squeezed all the same. My mother had sold many of our possessions before leaving Iran, but an unforgiving currency exchange rate meant that the proceeds didn't add up to much in dollars. As for paternal assistance, a few days before we were to depart, Parviz had dispatched Hadi to offer my mother a final installment of child support. He handed her an envelope containing about $10,000 in cash, but not before wagging his index finger in her face and warning her not to expect "a penny more than this—ever!"

Worried about depleting our funds, my mother bought a mobile home at a rundown trailer park on the outskirts of Logan. American homeownership for the sum of $3,000 was irresistible. The cultural meaning of living in a trailer park was initially lost on both of us. I wised up to it faster than she did, because I watched a lot more television. Americans who lived in mobile homes, I quickly gathered, tended to be ill-mannered and uneducated, the type who aired their dysfunctions on those tacky daytime shows.

I would rage at my poor mother: "That's not who we are, Niloofar! We have to move out!"

But what could she do? She was now a single mother, working graveyard shifts at a gas station while taking art classes during the day. She drove a 1980s-model Dodge pickup that was always on the verge of breaking down and frequently did. Yet, much as she had done in Iran, she tried to shield me from reality's blows. When I asked for that new book or music CD, she didn't object but quietly picked up the extra hours at work to pay for it. She bore constant witness to Balzac's maxim that women are born to suffer.

Things only got worse once I made friends at the high school. They were all outcasts, nerds, misfits of various sorts, which is why we connected in the first place. But even they lived in houses that couldn't be hitched to a truck and towed away. The poorest of them had concrete walls and decent furniture and proper yards that afforded real privacy. When they gave me rides home from school, I would ask them to drop me off a few blocks away, lest they find out where I lived; they all eventually discovered the truth.

How many times had Maman Farah assured me that I could trace my ancestry back at least seven generations through her side of the family? "All of them distinguished personages," she would say, "not one of them of low stock." Now we had transplanted our ancient and venerable roots, across the ocean, into a trailer park.

Our financial doldrums were one more knock against America. Yet the biggest affront of all was the existence and prominence in Utah of the Church of Jesus Christ of Latter-day Saints (LDS), also known as the Mormons.

My first encounter with the LDS faith came when my uncle's Mormon in-laws gave my mother and me a copy of the Book of Mormon. The mother-in-law had inscribed a note on the first page, entrusting us to God's care and urging us to seek solace in Jesus Christ. Neither my mother nor I cracked it open, and the book sat collecting dust in a corner of our bookshelf for months and years. Then one day I decided to tear it apart, first ripping the binding and then shredding the pages to bits.

No specific incident sparked this fit of anti-Mormon rage—or none that I can remember now. It was the culmination of a mounting hatred of Joseph Smith's religion and our neighbors who followed it with such sheepish obedience. By then I had concluded that the LDS faith was wackier and more implausible than Islam, and that living in a state with a distinct Mormon culture was as oppressive as living in an Islamic republic. "We've moved from one theocracy to another," I used to joke. It was an unfair, even obscene, comparison.

The Mormons maintained seminaries right next to most high schools, including mine, which I considered a grave violation of America's promise of secularity. Alcohol in beer was capped at 3 percent by state law—nothing like the mullahs' absolute prohibition, enforced on pain of flogging, but I drew the false equivalence anyway. Likewise, while there was no law in Utah against smoking or drinking coffee, LDS morality frowned on these minor vices. The Mormons shamed those who contravened their religious norms, coughing loudly as they walked by a smoker, for example, or holding forth loudly and publicly on the evils of caffeine.

"Man," I thought to myself, "at least the ayatollahs let you have your tea-and-a-cigarette in peace." I picked up smoking in these years, as a way to mark myself socially as a "gentile"—the LDS term for non-Mormons—and to punish those self-righteous scolds.

The Mormon family also drew my scorn. Typically, Mormons married young and had four or five children and sometimes more, in rapid succession. Weren't they just like those bumpkins in rural Iran, who jumped into arranged marriages at puberty and reproduced like rabbits? What kind of life was that, with the parents drowning under diapers and plastic toys before they had had the chance to achieve anything worthwhile? I came to suspect that the flirtatious Mormon girls at school, like those two cheerleaders, were really scheming to tie me down to an early marriage (as if I were such a magnificent catch at that age!).

To top it all, there was Mormon theology. I barely investigated their system, because I was uncurious and because what little I knew about it sufficed to convince me that it was a load of hooey. The LDS faith held that ancient Israelites had come to America, strove to convert the natives, and recounted their trials and New World revelations in golden tablets that form a sort of sequel to the Bible. The idea was so preposterous that it didn't deserve anything but mockery.*

* * * * *

When I entered junior year at Logan High School, I had all but abandoned that facile faith in America and the West, which I had nurtured from such an early age in Iran, and embraced the opposite extreme: a cantankerous, and equally facile, opposition to nearly everything about America and the West. Why was America, I wondered, beholden to the superstition and outmoded drivel of religion? Why did I hear so much talk about God? America

---

* Today, I admire a great deal in LDS culture and social teaching, and I wish more people in the West would emulate the Mormons in charity and in the defense of the natural family and the dignity of all human life. But my opinion of Mormon theology has remained unchanged.

was far from what it was cracked up to be. It was incumbent on me to skewer its ideals, much as I had begun to attack Islamic values under the mullahs.

My opinions were marked by an acute ignorance—about the Bible, about Judeo-Christianity and Western civilization, about American history and religion's place in it. But when did that ever stop teenagers from spouting their opinions?

Volatile emotions sloshed about inside me like an acidic mixture in an industrial vat. I poured out the pungent solution in daily conversation and into various poems, short stories, and many a novel abandoned on the first page. Typically, these early literary forays featured antiheroic protagonists, who wore upside-down crosses and engaged in ultraviolence. My embarrassing creations, which so appalled my classmates and teachers and brought me the attention I craved, were all derivative of third-rate horror movies and comic books. I thought they represented the height of originality.

I rejected out of hand nearly all efforts by adults to guide my energies. My mother, who knew something about art and aesthetics, I utterly cowed into submission. She was expected to instantly approve of whatever I came up with, lest I throw a teenage tantrum. Nor could she prevail upon me to heed others. An Iranian novelist, to whom she had mailed some of my literary efforts for critique, wrote back to say: "Your son needs, first, to read the Hebrew Bible before he can even begin to play around with Western ideas and symbols."

"Me? Read the outmoded superstition of the Bible? The man is insulting my intelligence!" I ripped his letter to shreds.

At school, I cultivated a gloomy persona and dressed in black every day: black denim, black combat boots, black

T-shirt, and black trench coat. I was overjoyed when, following months of entreaties on my part, the "goths" admitted me as a full member of their clique. These fellow malcontents dressed the same way (in black), watched the same shows, and shared the same antipathy for the "mainstream"—all in the name of nonconformity. In accord with the goth party line, my taste in music shifted from the heavily orchestrated and melodic Pink Floyd to the screeching vocals and brutal rhythms of Nine Inch Nails. I would blast NIN at earsplitting volumes on our stereo, taking satisfaction in shocking the neighbors' Mormon sensibilities.

Likewise, I would share my contrarian opinions with anyone willing to listen—and many who weren't. In social-studies class, I would stake out positions in favor of abortion and even postnatal infanticide, merely to get a rise. In English class, I pontificated at length on the sins of U.S. foreign policy, including on the day when Islamist hijackers rammed civilian airliners into the Twin Towers and the Pentagon. During recess, I drew mean caricatures of my classmates and circulated the sketches for the amusement of a few select friends.

All along, however, I remained the same high achiever that I had been in Iran. I got good grades; I took Advanced Placement courses; I thrived in extracurricular activities. My misdeeds never rose to a level that would have provoked a tough response from the school administration. I relied on my faux maturity and faux eloquence to skirt trouble and even win allies among the adults in the building. My conduct was disfiguring my character, yet there were no reckonings in store for me. With a little cleverness, it seemed, one could glide through American institutions. Only, I was gliding toward a life of permanent adolescence.

What saved me from that fate was reading.

Even as I drifted deeper into the goth subculture and its swamp of bad taste, a part of me knew, better than my conscious mind did, that this was a passing phase. It insisted, before my will was prepared to comply, that I should put away childish things (1 Cor 11:13). That intuition, or understanding before understanding, helped me retain a sense of vocation. I was still determined to be an intellectual of sorts, perhaps a professor of *something*. That, in turn, required me to become intimate with the printed word. I would remain thoughtless and insensible about most things, but I would read books that befitted my lofty aspirations.

But what to read? Well, I considered myself an ardent atheist. I had even taken to styling myself a "nihilist". My mother suggested that, if I was really wedded to these notions, I should explore the French existentialist writers: Albert Camus, Jean-Paul Sartre, and a few others. By appealing to my vanity, she chiseled away at the crust of arrogance around my mind. A few Internet searches later, and I had created an existentialist reading list. Baba Nasser proposed that I start a reading journal. This, too, I accepted, mainly because it involved buying new stationery. SOHRAB'S JOURNAL OF THEMATIC SUMMARY AND ANALYSIS was the portentous title I inscribed on the inside cover of the first black Moleskine.

Before I could get to the Frenchmen, however, I became acquainted with a German. Browsing the philosophy section of a bookstore in Salt Lake City during the summer before my senior year of high school, I came across a book by one Friedrich Wilhelm Nietzsche. On the dust jacket was a portrait of a brooding, *melan-cow-lick-* looking man with a receding hairline, thick eyebrows, and a mustache so bushy that it completely covered his mouth (it was a reproduction of Edvard Munch's 1906 portrait of Nietzsche). The book was titled *Thus Spoke Zarathustra*.

The scraps of information that I had gathered about him online disposed me well toward Nietzsche. That titular allusion to the ancient Persian proto-prophet Zoroaster was a nice bonus. I bought the book immediately. Little did I know that this exquisite hardcover would set me off on an intellectual and spiritual road that, years later, would bring me to a most unlikely destination: the Roman Catholic Church.

CHAPTER FIVE

THE ROAD FROM *ZARATHUSTRA*

Reading the great books in one's late teens is intoxicating. The critical faculties are half-formed at that age, liable to be overwhelmed by the literary master or virtuoso philosopher. The teenager reads each classic work thinking, "This book is so right!" and "Isn't it just so!"—without pausing to note the differences among the various authors, let alone his own doubts and objections. It was in this spirit of rash enthusiasm that I approached the existentialists, starting with Nietzsche.

To say that I "read" Nietzsche's *Thus Spoke Zarathustra* would be an understatement. I took the book home from the store, lay belly down on my bed, and finished it over three or four days, barely stepping out to eat and wash. I consumed *Zarathustra*, and it consumed me, in turn. Today I consider most of Nietzsche's ideas to be not merely wrong but positively sinister. His aphoristic style, which so wowed me at age sixteen, now strikes me as pretentious and overwrought. And yet he gave me the zest for philosophy and abstract ideas that has remained with me to this day.

Hitherto, I had only lashed out, crudely and feebly, at religion and authority. Reading Nietzsche lent me a conceptual framework for criticism and awakened me to the big questions: What is man? Where does he come from, and what is his destiny? What makes some men good and others bad? Is modern science capable of answering these questions? Or do we still need philosophy and ultimate truths to order and explain what our senses and instruments tell us?

He offered terrible answers. Following his *Zarathustra* led me, first, to some of the most lethal ideologies of the modern era and, later, to philosophies that denied the possibility of truth. Like some besotted intellectual groupie, I trailed Nietzsche and his Continental progeny wherever they led me. And like any fashion maven, I tried on every modish theory that I came upon along the way. None left me wiser than I was before.

* * * * *

"When Zarathustra was thirty years old he left his home and the lake of his home."

So began Nietzsche's madcap account of the life of his Zarathustra, a prophet come to herald a new epoch in human history and a new kind of man. When I first read it, I didn't even catch this opening allusion to the life of Jesus—the first of many throughout the book—for I hadn't yet read a single word of the Bible. Still, it didn't take a theologian to figure out that Zarathustra was on a warpath against God generally, and the God of the Bible especially.

Instead of commencing his public ministry at age thirty, as Christ did, Zarathustra goes "into the mountains" and spends ten years conversing with the sun and the moon, the trees and the birds. Then he descends into a nearby town, bringing news that God is dead.

That infamous proclamation sent a *frisson* of transgression down my spine. I reread the words several times: "God is dead." "God is dead." "*God is dead!*" Did that mean that God had been alive at some point? When had God died? Who had killed God? Or had God died of natural causes? It took some knowledge of the Western tradition—reaching back to Athens and Jerusalem and forward to the European Enlightenment—to truly appreciate Zarathustra's meaning. This was knowledge that I sorely lacked. Even on Nietzsche's own, militantly antitheistic terms, I was unprepared for the death of God.

In his first sermon, Zarathustra teaches that the great spirit who brings new values must first submit to the old. He must kneel "like a camel wanting to be well loaded". Only after becoming a beast of burden can this great spirit morph into the lion, which tears down every old value and every "thou shalt". Put another way: Only he who knows tradition through and through can destroy it. Afterward, the great spirit undergoes yet a third transformation: The ferocious lion must become a child, the bearer of the new.

I was not yet even the camel. But I pressed onward, drawn by the deceptively simple allegories and Zarathustra's roaring pronouncements, which, I thought, echoed the highest yearnings of my soul. What Zarathustra mainly spoke to was my loneliness. As Nietzsche's English translator and great booster, Walter Kaufmann, has noted, *Zarathustra* was the product of a supremely lonely mind, which is why the book has appealed to generations of alienated adolescents.

The Nietzschean prophet rages against the "believers of all faiths". Peeking behind their veil of piety and chastity, he discovers only hypocrisy, *ressentiment*, and the will to power. For Nietzsche, it is the will to power that animates all men and that is the wellspring of all morality. Different nations and character types through the ages have valued things differently, his Zarathustra says, according to their will to power and need for self-preservation. These valuations the various peoples have etched into tablets of moral law, hallowing their own invention as holy writ.

"Verily, men gave themselves all their good and evil," Zarathustra says. "Verily, they did not take it, they did not find it, nor did it come to them as a voice from heaven. Only man placed a value in things to preserve himself." Biblical morality reflects the will to power of slavelike men. Invented for and by people who envied the strong and the virile, it proscribes strength and virility. Invented for and by people who didn't appreciate earthly pleasures, it conditions men to fix their gaze on transcendent horizons.

"Isn't it just so!" I thought. Of course, a voice from heaven hadn't burst through the clouds to tell us, "Do this but not that." And hadn't Nietzsche described perfectly the conceit of the Mormon bishop and the gaudy televangelist, not to mention the Shiite ayatollah, who claimed to echo that voice from heaven? And wasn't *I* precisely the creative, virile type? Yes, and I had a right to seek my own way and my own values. But how was I supposed to do that? Here, Nietzsche's book took a mystical, and mystifying, turn.

Zarathustra prophesies the "overman". A series of revolutions in science and general knowledge—spurred, ironically, by Judeo-Christianity's exhortation to seek truth—has made God impossible. But men can't let go of him, or of parts of him; they still feel the tug of God's dead hand. Therefore, it is the all-too-human that must be overcome after God. Man must overcome himself, to give way to the overman. "Man is a rope," Zarathustra says, "tied between beast and overman—a rope over an abyss."

What an image! Was the overman, then, the end point of biological evolution? Was Nietzsche setting out a eugenic agenda? Not exactly, though assorted racists have long sought to claim him as their own. Nietzsche's thought was far too mad and anarchic to lend itself to such causes. He had no truck with the cult of Teutonic supremacy that was gathering strength in his lifetime and would go on to wreak global havoc a few decades after his death in 1900. And yet, there was no denying the elitism of his overman concept.

What distinguishes the overman from the all-too-human is the former's rejection of the good-and-evil mentality. This doesn't mean that there is no code or hierarchy of values: Zarathustra at various points sings hymns to self-mastery, true friendship, radical creativity. But for the overman, there are no preexisting moral absolutes that bind all. An action isn't inherently good or evil. Rather, what matters is *who* takes that action. The higher character type, the elevated soul, gives value to actions by virtue of the fact that he is higher.

The conclusion, which I drew but couldn't yet fully articulate, was that values were relative. What was wrong for the many was, perhaps, right for the few.

* * * * *

I drank *Thus Spoke Zarathustra* in my little room in our little trailer, and it proved a potent elixir. It healed some of the wounds of adolescent solitude even as it magnified my already-swollen sense of self-importance. Which clever and resentful teenager doesn't like to think of himself as ahead of the "superfluous many", as tending toward the overman while the rest are stuck in the all-too-human? *I don't need pep rallies and Christmastime food drives! I get to designate value, not the herd!*

Nietzsche corroborated all my prejudices against religion and traditional morality. The German philosopher wasn't the first to claim that all faith is but a fanciful tale that helps weak minds cope with the mystery of existence, or that organized religion is a con played by the hustling cleric on his gullible flock. But his genealogy of

Judeo-Christianity—that is, that it originates from a slave-like people's will to power—was unmatched for originality and polemical firepower. It struck me as perfectly cogent at the time.

With Nietzsche, I could be virulently misanthropic while claiming to stand for a deeper humanism than the religious believer could appreciate. The Nietzschean spirit locked his gaze on the horizon of the here and now—on what he could achieve within the bounds of his own reason, creativity, love, and will to power. Wasn't that a more humane, more heroic spirituality than one that sought after an invisible, all-seeing, all-judging deity in the sky?

Then, too, Nietzsche pinpointed exactly what it was that I had found so dissatisfying about America. Although he reserved most of his bile for religion, he was also a vicious critic of egalitarian liberalism. When I lived in a society animated by romantic politics and Islamic messianism, the West was my lodestar, because it stood for science, progress, equality of the sexes, and so on. When I crossed the ocean and saw liberal modernity up close, however, there was no denying that something was amiss.

Enter Zarathustra. Nietzsche's prophet despises modernity's "last men", who boast: "We have invented happiness." Theirs is a sterile, gray happiness. For the last men, there is no darkness and therefore no light; work is entertainment, and vice versa; and everyone is more or less the same—everyone is equal. "One has one's little pleasure for the day and one's little pleasure for the night," they say.

Didn't America—with its frozen burritos and vulgar shows and egalitarian ethos—exemplify the kind of emptiness Nietzsche decried? Americans disagreed vehemently about unimportant things: the weather, cars, football. But when it came to the most important questions, they kept disagreements to a minimum, if they didn't keep mum altogether. Yes, America was the home of the last men. But what about its religiosity? Didn't that suggest that there was more to America than endless banality?

Ah, but here Nietzsche made his cleverest move yet. The world of the last men, he said, had come about when two streams merged. One was the stream of biblical religion; the other, egalitarian liberalism. The latter claimed a rupture with the former. But liberalism was an extension of biblical religion. It was from Judeo-Christianity that the liberal-egalitarians had received their egalitarianism, their pity for the poor and the lame, their universalist notions of justice and fairness. The last men were high on the fumes of the slave morality.

To be a Nietzschean, then, was to fight on two fronts, against the liberal-egalitarian last men and the remnants of biblical religion. I was ready to enlist. Alas, there was no Party of Nietzsche accepting recruits in Logan, Utah. So I did next best thing, which was to major in philosophy upon graduating high school. At the time, Utah State University offered full rides, with generous stipends, to the winners of its annual humanities essay contest. I submitted an essay expounding my newfound Nietzschean convictions; it won in the philosophy category. This was no small blessing. Though our financial picture was slowly improving, attending college out of state was yet inconceivable.

* * * * *

I didn't really go to college, if by "college" is meant a course of preparation for self-government and the examined life. I did go to college, however, in the sense that I attended some classes, first at Utah State University and later at the University of Washington in Seattle; took exams and wrote final papers; did drugs and drank far too much; hooked up randomly if not frequently; and was eventually awarded a degree in philosophy.

The blame for my fruitless university career belongs to me. Although my undergraduate alma maters weren't top-flight schools, they offered plenty of opportunities for genuine learning, including from some truly exceptional scholars. The trouble was that I entered college convinced that I already knew everything there was to know. The point of higher education, I thought, was to reaffirm and broadcast my own ideas.

Once more, I glided through and, judging by grades, even had a splendid education. My "success" owed mainly to my swift mastery of the art of college writing. I could draft sensible prose or, when necessary, imitate postmodern Academese and hide my intellectual laziness under thick layers of gobbledygook. I suffered from the worst kind of ignorance in college, the kind that is papered over with little bits of erudition and the occasional striking phrase. I didn't even know what I didn't know.

How I wish one of my professors had told me: "No, you are writing shallow nonsense. You need to go back, read such and such, really think this problem through." Or how I wish there had been a course that would have required me to study the great books, closely and carefully, in some logical order. I doubt that I would have heeded such advice or taken such opportunities, however, even if they had come my way. I arrived on campus with a syllabus of my own, as it were, and the professors were content to let me work through it independently.

Having read much of Nietzsche's oeuvre in high school, I turned next to the other existentialists: Albert Camus and Jean-Paul Sartre mainly but also Søren Kierkegaard, Fyodor Dostoevsky, Franz Kafka, Georges Bataille, Hermann Hesse, and Eugène Ionesco. I treated these authors as if

they all belonged to a single, cohesive intellectual movement that shared the same beliefs about everything. I pos-
ited an existentialist ideology where none existed. Some
of these writers had died before the term "existentialism"
had even been coined, while others explicitly rejected
the appellation.

Still, there was a certain mood of anxiety or despair
that tied together the existentialist philosophers and the
existential-ish novelists and playwrights. All of them grap-
pled with the consequences of "a world divested of meaning", as I might have written in one of my college essays.
Kierkegaard and Dostoevsky were Christians. But even
for them, God's presence was obscured, either because a
"chasmic abyss" separated men from the divine (the Dane),
or because modern man had tried to make a god of himself
(the Russian).

More typical, and more in accord with my own thinking, was Camus' and Sartre's insistence that there is no God
and therefore that human existence has no metaphysical
origin, no destination. "Existence before essence" was Sartre's handy, if oversimplified, definition of existentialism.
Starting from that premise, the two took different paths,
morally and politically, a divergence that would eventually
put an end to their personal friendship. Faced with the
Camus-Sartre fork in the existentialist road, I initially went
the way of Camus.

His 1942 novel, *The Stranger*, was another one of those
adolescent masterpieces. It tells of a *pied-noir* in colonial
Algeria who shoots and kills an Arab for no good reason other than that the sun's glare irritates his eyes. Tried
and sentenced to death, Camus' protagonist, Meursault,
remains unrepentant. His moral indifference flows from
the "gentle indifference of the world", as he puts it in his
final soliloquy before his execution.

The Stranger painted a bleak picture of modern man's moral and spiritual landscape. But it was clear that Camus the philosopher didn't prescribe such monstrous indifference. His point, elucidated in essays such as "The Myth of Sisyphus" (1942), was that the inevitability of death rendered human existence absurd. Like the mythical Sisyphus, men spent their days toiling against death, only for the boulder to roll back down the mountainside at night, for death to have the final say. Yet human life's absurdity and fragility lent existence a precious dignity. It was necessary to uphold that dignity, Camus argued, through the ethical exercise of the free will.

For Camus, the morally exemplary man par excellence was the physician who treats patients amid an outbreak of the plague, knowing well he might contract the disease and, moreover, that death renders his good actions ultimately pointless. I am describing, of course, Dr. Bernard Rieux, the protagonist of Camus' other major novel, *The Plague*, from 1947. Pressed by a friend about why he displays such devotion to his patients, though he is an unbeliever, Dr. Rieux answers: "Since the order of the world is shaped by death, mightn't it be better for God if we refuse to believe in him and struggle with all our might against death, without even raising our eyes toward the heaven where he sits in silence?"

For a little while, I adopted this existential humanism à la Rieux as my personal code. I liked to think that I was modeling my life after the doctor's—that, if faced with a mass catastrophe of some sort, I would act heroically, in the full knowledge that my actions would mean nothing in the grand scheme of things. Needless to say, it was easy to think such pleasant thoughts about myself when there was no outbreak of disease or fascist takeover—the plague is also a political metaphor—to test my moral mettle.

Meanwhile, I was as selfish as ever when it came to more quotidian moral choices.

Eventually, I traded Camus and his heroic physician for Sartre. The other Frenchman had grander ideas about moral and political commitment in a world without God. Sartre was an ardent Communist. For him, it was class struggle that opened the way to man's true ground of freedom. Now here was a concrete political project I could sign up for.

He was hardly the only French philosopher of his generation to abandon himself to the Communist cause. With a very few exceptions—Camus among them, hence his rupture with Sartre—Parisian intellectuals postwar looked with admiration to the Marxist experiments in the Soviet Union, China, Cuba, and elsewhere. Communist regimes, they believed, had broken the shackles of alienation that had bound men since time immemorial. They maintained this faith in the socialist ideal, even as evidence mounted of the inhumanity of actually existing socialism.

Sartre was an especially abject apologist, an expert at passing off slavish defense of Moscow as moral sophistication. Take his play *Dirty Hands*. The protagonist is an idealistic Communist intellectual, Hugo, whose "bourgeois morality" prevents him from seeing why the party has to forge an alliance with fascist forces in a fictional country in Eastern Europe (much as Joseph Stalin had done with the real-world Molotov-Ribbentrop Pact). Hugo is a foil to Hoederer, the charismatic, hardened party apparatchik, who loves "men for what they are" and therefore has no use for idealism. The veteran party man understands that you can't wage class warfare, and liberate the human race, without getting your hands dirty.

It was obvious which of the two types Sartre thought was up to the responsibilities of the twentieth century. The

Hoederer posture—anti-idealism in the name of a deeper idealism, immorality in service of a truer morality—was that of the political fanatic, who is prepared to excuse any crime and violate any principle to bring about utopia, as Sartre indeed was. But how did Sartre square existentialism's individualistic, lone-man-against-the-void vibe with Marxism-Leninism? For that matter, how did I get over Nietzsche's anti-egalitarian grumblings, which I had taken to heart, and champion an ideology that called for the leveling of all class differences?

Easily. Nietzschean existentialism considered man to be his own moral measure, and it licensed an elite to designate new values and overthrow the old. Communism—a movement led by intellectuals, in the name and at the expense of workers—did just that. Which was why I didn't bat an eye when Marxism-Leninism presented itself as the next step after existentialism. By the age of eighteen, I was quite literally a card-carrying Communist.

* * * * *

"Hello?"

"Yes, hello, um, is this Worker's Alliance? I want to, um, join your organization."

It was an inauspicious start to my career in Marxist politics. Having resolved to dedicate myself to overthrowing capitalism, I went online in search of hard-left organizations in Utah—there weren't that many—and picked the only one that appeared to consist of more than one cranky fellow operating out of a dank basement.

The outfit, Worker's Alliance, was the American branch of a global organization known as the World Congress of the Fourth International. Ideologically, the Alliance and WCFI were Trotskyite—that is, they drew inspiration from Leon Trotsky, the Russian revolutionary and martyr

to Stalinism. This alleviated somewhat my mother's appre-
hensions about my Communist turn. She had no love for
Communism, but to her mind Trotsky had been the one
good guy in the whole sordid business.

According to a myth cultivated by his Western followers, Trotsky was a friend to artists and a gentle man of letters, who might have built a more humane USSR had he
survived Stalin's depredations. In fact, Trotsky had been
as cruel as any of the other leading Bolsheviks before Stalin sidelined him. Yet such was my fervor that I didn't
permit myself to read an objective history of the October
Revolution and its aftermath. Instead, I plowed through
Isaac Deutscher's three-volume hagiography of Trotsky,
The Prophet. Hot tears filled my eyes when I reached the
final pages, which told of how the old man had resisted
Stalinism to the last, struggling for hours after an assassin
had buried an ice ax two inches into his skull at the behest
of the Kremlin.

I wept for a Soviet leader, and became insufferably
self-righteous.

The voice on the other end of the line introduced himself
as John Smyth ("with a *y*"). He sounded hesitant at first, as
if my straightforward request to join his group had caught
him off-guard, but once his Marxist zeal kicked in, I couldn't
get a word in edgewise. Ours was a critical moment for
developing socialism "in this country", he said, what with
the "whole system" in crisis—this was a year after 9/11—
and the "forces of capital" no longer able to contain capitalism's "internal contradictions". And could I come down to
Salt Lake City for some important meetings?

I felt as though I was about to be inducted into a select
group that had advance knowledge of the twists and turns
of world history before they unfolded. That was precisely
what all Communist parties claimed to possess. The key

to unlocking this secret knowledge was dialectical materialism. It was a "science of history", first developed by Karl Marx, that helped the party analyze and predict social change based on the modes and relations of production—that is, how things were produced and who owned the means of production.

Class struggle, according to this theory, was the engine of history. Every age hitherto had been marked by antagonism between social classes, and the modern one was no different. Capitalism, our enemy, had pitilessly destroyed older social forms—good riddance to feudalism and superstition!—and concentrated the factories, firms, and banks in the hands of a greedy few. Everyone else it had reduced to wage slavery. Workers produced the real value, yet the capitalist system alienated them from the fruit of their labor. The stage was set for massive upheaval.

Only, the workers suffered from "false consciousness". The system hoodwinked them into believing that their interests were aligned with the bosses'; that they were "free" because they retained "bourgeois rights" like free speech and due process; or else that they should await the kingdom of heaven rather than take power on earth. The workers weren't up for revolution. They were a class "in themselves but not for themselves", in Marx' famous expression. Thus, it was up to professional revolutionaries to act as their "vanguard".

Toward the end of freshman year, I drove my new Honda Civic to Salt Lake, where I was to meet the Worker's Alliance crew. I had purchased the car with earnings from a part-time market research job. That fact alone illustrated that capitalism in America in 2003 had little to do with the smoggy, grinding Victorian Manchester that had served as Marx' muse and laboratory. But I wasn't wise enough yet to judge theory against life experience.

The address I had took me to a quiet neighborhood on the outskirts of Salt Lake. There, in a modest duplex, a suburban vanguard fantasized about restaging the *Ten Days That Shook the World*. Smyth greeted me at the door. He must have been in his thirties. He had a limp leg and one eye that was permanently shut and another that bulged out of its socket; various tics convulsed his body every few minutes. Smyth was the practical one. He scouted for recruits, communicated with headquarters in Seattle, represented the party at strikes and protests. In between, he worked at a customer-support call center for a tech company.

His deputy was Markus Van Doren, a forty-something Flemish mathematics lecturer straight out of central casting for Eccentric Marxist Professor. Van Doren had an encyclopedic grasp of the Marxist canon, and he existed in a state of permanent disputation with other theorists, most long dead, over the correct interpretation of, say, Marx' *Eighteenth Brumaire of Louis Bonaparte* or Trotsky's *Transitional Program*. Eating, drinking, socializing, his day job—these were all distractions, which he unfortunately had to put up with. He owned the duplex with a long-suffering wife, whom I would often catch glancing at her husband and his weirdo friends with a look that combined pity and fury in equal measure.

The third member—I would join as a fourth—was Derek. He was a teenage runaway who had dropped out of high school and spent the nights in shelters. Unlike the rest of us, Derek really was dispossessed, and we appreciated his comradeship all the more for that. But I don't recall us ever doing much to help improve his lot. Then again, spreading goodwill, making human connections, acting charitably—these were ideological constructs that helped perpetuate the system. Charity blunted social antagonisms, when the Marxist's task was to sharpen them.

We aggressively hawked the latest issues of our newspaper, *Equity*, which each week told the same stories in slightly repackaged form: Capitalism is in crisis; globalization is a scam; the two major parties are beholden to the same corporate masters. If we got word of a strike action at some Utah mine, we would race to join in. We stuck out like sore thumbs on the picket, but the miners welcomed us, and it was stirring to join our voices to their chants: "Hey-hey! Ho-ho! Corporate greed has got to go!"; "What time is it? UNION TIME!"

Then there were the monthly meetings. Smyth and Van Doren ran these according to the Leninist principle of democratic centralism: Disagreement was allowed until a decision was reached, at which point the minority was required to set aside its reservations and endorse the majority position wholeheartedly. Not that there was much disagreement. Whatever the social ill under discussion on a given night—unemployment, poverty, war, environmental degradation—we all concurred that it ultimately traced back to capitalism.

It didn't matter that our endless talk didn't solve any problems. We knew that the classless society was the preordained end point of human history. The dialectic would turn and turn until the final triumph of Communism. Gathered in Van Doren's study or the hipster cafés of Salt Lake, we few were nudging history toward its final destination.

* * * * *

When I dabbled in Marxism, a decade after the end of the Cold War, the ideology had been utterly discredited. Contrary to Marx' predictions, capitalism hadn't pauperized workers in the advanced industrial countries. Instead, it had spawned middle classes across the West, people whose material prosperity disinclined them to revolution. Communism had gained a foothold only in undeveloped, agricultural lands like Russia and China—and there, only thanks to the bloody methods of the various Communist parties. Wherever Marx' economic ideas had been implemented, the gulag, the killing field, the torture chamber, and the man-made famine were never far behind.

Why, then, did I cling to Marxism for years?

The thrill of *épater les bourgeois* surely had something to do with it. In Utah in those days, identifying as a plain old Democrat marked one as an exotic bird. To espouse Marxism—the ideology of the late, unmourned Evil Empire—was that much more countercultural and, I thought, cool. I remembered how, back in Iran, when one spoke of an intellectual, it was automatically assumed that one meant a *chapi*, a "leftist". Thus, I ended up once more borrowing someone else's identity in service of a dubious individuality.

There were other layers. My childish Americanism, you will recall, was made of light stuff. Faced with America as it really was, it quickly morphed into anti-Americanism. With Marxism, I could oppose the United States as the evil, capitalist hegemon without having to buy into any of the Shiite mumbo jumbo from the old country. Growing up in a totalitarian society, it turned out, didn't inoculate me against other totalitarian temptations. Marxism, moreover, assuaged my class anxieties: My economic displacement— from a doted-upon son of Iran's middle class to a trailer-park kid—was but a ripple in the dialectic.

Analytically speaking, Marxism was a useful instrument for a young would-be intellectual. Social class was a significant factor in the lives of people everywhere and at all times, and this meant that the application of Marxist methods to, say, the study of the French novel or Hindu religion or what have you could yield some clever insights. It was satisfying to read a classic, not on its own terms, but as a mirror held up to the economic dynamics of its period, the author's social class, and so on. Nothing was true for all times and for all people. Everything was historical; everything could be historicized. I retained this Marxist habit of mind—soulless, reductionist, and terribly wrong— long after I left the ideology behind.

Yet Marxism's greatest attraction was its religious spirit. In those days I couldn't see how the materialist dialectic and the Marxist science of history were really "secularized theologies", as the liberal French philosopher Raymond Aron had argued in the 1950s. But I *felt* in my heart the poetry and metaphysics of Marxism's secular salvation story, in which history designated the revolutionary party as mankind's savior. In the Marxist imagination, revolutionary sacrifice would consummate and redeem, violently and spectacularly, every injustice and every tragedy through the ages. History would wipe away every tear.

God was supposed to be dead, yet I was still grasping for him on the darkened road from *Zarathustra*.

CHAPTER SIX

DIVINE CONDESCENSION

I moved out of my mother's after freshman year and rented a room in an apartment building just off campus. The three-story complex was something of a student slum. My unit, on the top floor, had sticky linoleum flooring, cheap broken fixtures, and inoperable air conditioning that left it baking in the dry heat of the Utah summer. I didn't mind, though. It was better than that ignominious trailer park, and I reveled in the new freedom that came with flying out of the maternal nest.

Only, now I had to put up with a pair of Mormon roommates, just back from their missions abroad to attend Utah State. Or, to be more precise, they had to put up with me. The two were athletic, polite, upstanding young men, with identical faded buzz cuts and a shared fondness for plaid shirts and khaki utility pants. Their friendly, cheerful mien—"Hiya, Sohrab! How was your day today?"—was grating. How could anyone be so chipper, so indifferent to superexploitation and imperialist wars?

Nick and Taylor—or Tweedledee and Tweedledum, as I hatefully nicknamed them—mostly kept to themselves and, contrary to the Mormon stereotype, made no effort to convert me to their religion. It was I who went out of my way to stick my non-Mormon ways in their faces. Smokers were required to go down to the parking lot, but I lit up on the balcony, next to their windows. Alcohol was prohibited, but I invited my old high school buddies to drink in my room. I never missed a chance to cuss within my roomies' earshot.

I also made a point of reading in the living area, rather than privately in my room, and deliberately left my books sitting out in the shared spaces. It would benefit those ignorant hicks, I thought, to discover that there is more to the world of letters than their Bible and Mormon study books. (What a vain, fatuous creature I was!)

In those days, my literary diet still consisted mainly of Marxist books. To clear my palate from time to time, I took to reading the Beat Generation. Allen Ginsberg, Jack Kerouac, Neal Cassady, and William S. Burroughs were rebels of a different sort than Nietzsche or Marx. The Beats were eclectic, wild, and homegrown American. I was as much fascinated by their dissolute lives as by their prose and verse. The Beats, it seemed to me, had transfigured their debauchery into an authentic style. Perhaps I could do the same.

"Authenticity" was the lodestone I picked up from the Beats. My sense of what it meant was as hazy as the earlier "modern" and "rational". Debauchery was the height of authenticity. People were their truest selves when they gave in to the kind of moral looseness that marked Kerouac's and Cassady's travels in *On the Road*. If that was true, then my buddies and I were on to something when we shared a handle of vodka and exchanged pseudoprofundities for hours in the woods of Logan Canyon. Surrounded by the limestone cliffs and sheltered under a canopy of junipers and firs, we would unsettle our minds with booze and weed, now rejoicing at the secret knowledge we thought these intoxicants afforded, now quivering with fear of arrest, now surrendering to sleep amid the grass and alpine wildflowers.

One thing was certain: sobriety, manners, order—these were repressive barriers that had to be broken with the help of strong drink and mind-altering drugs. In a society founded on Puritanical conformity, to drink hard and do drugs was a bold political statement. (Perhaps my father really was influencing me telepathically from across the ocean.) If only I had known that in America in 2003, self-indulgence was the norm, and self-denial the countercultural act par excellence.

*　*　*　*　*

It was my copy of Burroughs' *Naked Lunch* that I most fervently wished my Mormon roommates would pick up after I "accidentally" laid it about our living room. I pictured the revulsion on their faces when they flipped through page after page of profane prose and surreal, grotesque imagery: a man whose sentient backside takes control of his body and seals off his mouth; sadomasochistic torture, homosexual orgies, and heroin trips in hellish alternate dimensions; and much else of the kind that led to the book being banned in Boston in 1962.

My roommates' picking up the book never came to pass—or if it did, I never found out. But the exact opposite of what I had planned *did* take place during our second semester together. One day, while they were out to class, I came across a leather-bound King James Bible that one or the other had left on our couch. I was bored, so I stepped out to the balcony for a smoke. When I came back inside, I threw myself down on the couch, opened the Bible to the New Testament, and read the Gospel of Saint Matthew in one go.

I can't say that the first twenty-five chapters made much of an impression on me. My frame of mind was contemptuous. "Here we go with the hocus-pocus, blah-blah, Jesus is born, blah-blah, Jesus tells a parable, blah-blah, Jesus performs a miracle, blah-blah, another parable," was how I read the portions of the Gospel that Matthew devotes to Christ's life and ministry. But that changed when I got to chapter 26, which is to say, to the Passion narrative.

I remember sitting up and reading attentively, where before I had been perusing languidly. Against my every inclination and instinct, the evangelist's account of the suffering and crucifixion of Jesus had me transfixed. "And it came to pass, when Jesus had finished all these sayings, he said unto his disciples, Ye know that after two days is the feast of the passover, and the Son of man is betrayed to be crucified" (Mt 26:1–2, KJV).

Two simple verses crystallized the double tragedy of the Passion. First, evil men betray, condemn, torture, and execute an innocent man. Now, as a Marxist, I might have told myself that all morality and laws are historically contingent—that good and evil, or licit and illicit, reflect the preferences of the owner class at every time and in every culture. I might have held, therefore, that true justice lies in reordering society and leveling all disparities, so that there are no more owners and no more dispossessed. But the fact of *this* particular injustice, done to *this* particular man at *this* particular time, was inescapable.

Maybe I wasn't such a good Marxist. The true student of the science of history, I knew, looks upon the injustices of the past with coldly analytical eyes and ironic detachment. The German Jewish theorist Walter Benjamin captured the properly historicist attitude in his essay "On the Concept of History". He wrote it in 1940, amid the eruption of bloodletting in Europe that would claim his own life the same year (Benjamin committed suicide at the French-Spanish border while trying to escape the Nazis).

In it, Benjamin meditated on the "new angel" depicted in Paul Klee's painting *Angelus Novus*. The angel's "eyes are opened wide," he wrote, "his mouth stands open and his wings are outstretched. The Angel of History must look just so. His face is turned towards the past. Where *we* see the appearance of a chain of events, *he* sees one single catastrophe, which unceasingly piles rubble on top of rubble." The angel would like to pause, to take stock of the damage, to repair the broken bodies, classes, and nations heaped on the pile, but alas, "a storm is blowing from Paradise," and the gusts propel him in the opposite direction, toward the future.

The persecution and killing of a Jewish man two thousand years earlier amounted to a speck of dust in the enormous heap of rubble kicked up by the dialectical storm. It was nothing next to the injustices suffered by multitudes who had toiled under various regimes of exploitation, only to perish unknown and unheralded. Or next to such marquee modern calamities as the Napoleonic Wars and the two World Wars. Next to Auschwitz and Hiroshima. (Never mind the many millions slaughtered by Marxist regimes.) The Marxist takes in the whole pile unflinchingly. He knows that history works in and through these tragedies, to bring each age to its fullness and prepare the way for the next. As Benjamin put it: "That which we call progress, is *this* storm."

And yet, my mind protested, here is *one* good man unjustly put to death—a man whose nobility is apparent even to his executioners (Mt 27:14). I should note that I didn't fully grasp the divinity of Jesus, nor would I have been prepared to accept it, had I understood it. I was an atheist, yes, but I also held onto certain fragments of my Islamic education. Muslims venerate Jesus as one in a long line of God's messengers and the second-greatest prophet after Muhammad. But in Islam, Jesus isn't God or the Son of God. *Lam yaled wa lam yulad* (God neither begat nor was begotten), taught the Qur'an. One can disavow a religion or an idea and still cling to its prejudices.

Still, I had to admit that the Jesus portrayed by Matthew is an extraordinary figure, not least because—and this is the second dimension of the twofold tragedy—he submits willingly to the injustice meted out to him. When one of his friends takes up arms to defend him against his enemies, he commands him: "Put up again thy sword into his place: for all they that take the sword shall perish with the sword" (Mt 26:52, KJV). He could call at any time on armies of angels to protect him, he says, yet he doesn't (Mt 26:53). As he hangs from the Cross, his persecutors mock him: Rescue yourself if you are who you say you are (Mt 27:40–43)! He doesn't rebuke them but suffers in silence (Mt 27:44).

When the strong torment the weak, we pity the latter and are outraged by the former. The martyrdom of Imam Hussein was the quintessential example of this. At Karbala, the hypocrites outnumbered the righteous, thirty thousand to seventy-two. The imam and his companions fought valiantly to the last drop of blood, before the Yazidians snuffed out their lives and cause. But the Passion of Christ is radically different. On the Cross, it is the strong one who condescends to the weak and evil many. He *allows* them to persecute him.

This Great Reversal was startling—and unspeakably beautiful. But why? What made Christ's total surrender, when he could have vanquished his enemies in an instance (Mt. 27:51), so touching, even to an unbeliever? What was it about sacrifice, whether Hussein's or Jesus', that left such a searing imprint on my mind? Why did I long for sacrifice? These questions stayed with me for many years after reading Saint Matthew's Gospel.

I don't mean to make too much of my first encounter with Scripture. The Passion gripped me as narrative, but I was hostile to its cosmic meaning. And when I reached the Resurrection of Christ, my skepticism returned in full force. Of course, a dead man can't return to life, I thought. What unadulterated hokum. The Resurrection was just another iteration of the all-too-human dream of defying mortality.

It would be half a decade or more before I would even begin to reconsider my atheism and still longer before I would consider myself a Christian. At the moment, I closed my roommate's Bible thinking that, although Christianity was surely as false as every other religion, it couldn't easily be dismissed; there was *something* in the myth of Christ's sacrifice that transcended history and class struggle.

* * * * *

I transferred to the University of Washington at the end of that academic year (my second), to be closer to Worker's Alliance's headquarters in Seattle. I also figured that it would benefit my future career—perhaps a professorship in philosophy or cultural studies—if I earned my degree from a higher-ranked university, though I had already completed most of the credits needed for a bachelor of arts in philosophy at Utah State.

In the spring of 2004, I flew to Seattle in search of class prestige and the classless society. I was nineteen. Academically, I continued to follow my personal syllabus at UW. But I relished the chance to stretch my city-boy legs, which had atrophied after years spent in the small towns of the Mountain West. The rain-drenched Emerald City offered plenty of amusements, high and low. I scooped up as much of it as I could: the Antonin Artaud production as well as the wild frat party, the contemporary-art exhibit as well as the punk rock concert. Mostly I played at leftist politics.

It was a time of ideological ferment. A year had gone by since the United States–led invasion of Iraq. The death toll continued to rise, and it was clear that America couldn't extricate itself from the Mesopotamian quicksand anytime soon. Seattle, especially, was a hotbed of hard-left activism. Memories of massive riots targeting a gathering of the World Trade Organization five years earlier were fresh on the minds of the city's left-wing activists. George W. Bush's post-9/11 wars, they hoped, would spark even bigger protests and swell their ranks with new members.

I sought out the comrades right away. In Seattle, Worker's Alliance maintained an expansive house near the UW campus, where the core leadership lived and worked. There was Paul, the party's spokesman, whose charisma defied his perfectly bald head and high-pitched, nasal speech. Tarek, a soft-spoken young Arab American who had been a college classmate of Paul's, edited *Equity*. The two were, I think, in their late twenties or early thirties. The rest of us were much younger, and included not a few attractive but rather severe young women. With these last I tried but couldn't make a connection beyond the strictly world-historical task at hand.

The operation was, on the whole, professional, and the city's progressive bent meant that socialist activism was a more fruitful enterprise here than it had been in Utah. Students attended our rallies in relatively large numbers. *Equity* sold well. The only thing that seemed to be missing was the working class, whose mantle the party claimed. Though I didn't give it much thought then, it was obvious that the full-time socialist life was possible only for the children of the upper-middle class. Paul and Tarek, for example, had both attended Oberlin, the elite liberal arts college in Ohio.

Yet it wasn't the unspoken elitism that ultimately repelled me from the party. Rather, it was the obsessive mono-thought and claims of omniscience—the very things that had attracted me to Worker's Alliance in the first place. Paul, Tarek, and crew were singularly devoted to developing "cadres", young idealists whom they would fashion into identical versions of themselves, down to the way they spoke. I was a potential cadre, which, I suspected, was why Tarek would pester me nonstop for one-on-one meetings. The point was to persuade me, through rote repetition, that Worker's Alliance had the answer to nearly everything.

We usually met on "the Ave", the row of student bars, tattoo parlors, and record shops that abutted the main UW campus. Tarek would start by reviewing the day's headlines, which back then (as now) were often dominated by the scourge of jihadism. It was a topic I knew something about, having lived under the world's first modern Islamist regime. Tarek would put down the party line: Islamism was an outgrowth of class tensions inside Middle Eastern societies.

"Here's what we do know," he would say, in a didactic tone that chafed me to no end. "It's impossible to understand this fundamentalist moment without figuring out the economic and social conditions in places like Iraq and Egypt or in your country."

"Right."

"Do you remember how Marx described religion?"

"The sigh of the oppressed? The opium of the masses?"

"Precisely. These are people who don't hold any worldly hope. So without a secular socialist movement, who can speak for them but the mullahs and the muftis?"

"Right."

The substance of faith was irrelevant to us, he explained. Islam isn't any more radical or reactionary than any other religion. The positive stuff of any religion turns on the economy and the class interests of the clerics. And these can change. Depending on the social and economic balance of forces, Islamism can be an anti-imperialist force, or it can be a tool for capital and imperialism. "Right?"

"Right."

"Right? So, for us, in the long view, it's the working class that holds the key to progressive change."

"Right."

His was an outlook on life that I still broadly shared. I had espoused the same materialist ideas countless times and in various forms. In my Nietzschean days, I believed that the weak and "superfluous many" had invented religion to tie down the strong few. As a Marxist, I held the opposite: that the wealthy few had invented religion to pacify the dispossessed many.

Yet I was becoming dimly aware that that wasn't true—or rather, that it wasn't the whole truth. I lacked a solid foundation of philosophical training to help me withstand Tarek's carefully rehearsed arguments, hence my dutiful affirmations. But it was enough that I found strict dialectical materialism intellectually stifling. Trotskyites could be as zealous and fanatical as any religious fundamentalist. Their dourness, their indifference to anything outside their ideological bubble, their endless internecine rivalries with other Marxist groupuscules—all this reminded me of the Khomeinists of my childhood.

How had I wound up among the fanatics once more, this time by choice? I had set out on the road from *Zarathustra* seeking the freedom that, I imagined, would be found on the far side of the death of God. I wanted to liberate myself from every ancient authority and every "thou shalt". And yet here I was, caught up in an ideology that narrowly constricted the range of permissible thoughts and questions. My mind was now in thrall to a system that radically subordinated the self to the collective and the political party.

Had I taken a wrong turn somewhere beyond the ramparts of monotheism?

If I were wise, these second thoughts would have led me back to the drawing board, so to speak. I would have taken the opportunity to study what those ancient authorities had to say before dismissing them out of hand. I would have returned to the first questions—about human nature, good and evil, the relationship between empirical fact and truth, and so on—which I had never really explored, taking on faith the answers offered by Nietzsche and his progeny.

I was not wise. I was taking courses on classical philosophy, the mind-body problem, and even Protestant theology at UW. The texts, whether Plato's *Timaeus* or Paul Tillich's *Systematic Theology*, could have nudged me in the right direction, had I approached them with an open mind. But I was sure that any book that predated Marx and Nietzsche, or that drew on the Bible, was bound to be incorrect. Materialism had already conquered those old ideas—what was the point of engaging with the intellectual equivalent of museum pieces? I would pompously lecture my professors on these points. Inexplicably, they let me get away with it and even awarded me high marks.

Yet my ideological prejudices were themselves in flux. For as I say, I had had it with the Trotskyites. Could any reasonable person expect soviets and proletarian dictatorship to make a comeback in our time? (I couldn't be sure that Tarek, Paul, and the rest counted as reasonable.) I still admired the great Marxist thinkers, to be sure. But most of them had both feet firmly planted in the nineteenth century, in a world of iron, coal, and steam, of orphaned chimney sweepers and metal lunch buckets—a world that had all but vanished, in other words.

Marx, Lenin, and Trotsky never imagined today's hyperconnected, digital world (Facebook had just appeared around this time). Nor did they have much to say about those other aspects of human identity that were now at the forefront of the progressive mind—namely, race, gender, and sexuality. In short, I was now poised to take the leap from orthodox Marxism toward post-structuralism and postmodernism that leftist "critical theory" had taken beginning in the 1960s and '70s.

In my dorm room, I hoarded books by the likes of Jean Baudrillard, Jean-François Lyotard, Judith Butler, and Michel Foucault. These thinkers wrote prose that was more abstruse and impenetrable than even Marx', surely a sign that they were on to something deep. Plus, they took on sex and gender, language and the unconscious, colonialism and postcolonialism, media and pop culture— subjects that were more pertinent, and more titillating, to a young millennial immigrant in Seattle than old Marxist standbys like surplus profit and the labor theory of value.

In winter 2005, I wrote a scathing e-mail to Tarek, announcing my departure from Worker's Alliance on the grounds that the party paid insufficient attention to the discoveries of the postmodernists. I exchanged one mess of pottage for another.

* * * * *

When I was twenty years old and on the verge of graduating college, my worldview was a welter of resentment, confusion, and ideological crankery. If I were to boil it down to a single idea, it would be this: Man's place in the world is unsettled; he is homeless. Capitalism's pitiless destruction of older social forms, Charles Darwin's theory of evolution, Freud's discovery of the unconscious—all these things had made it impossible to cling to any eternal or permanent truth about humanity. The ancient prophets and philosophers had deluded themselves. Everything about people turned on historical conditions and social power dynamics.

My new postmodern idols claimed a rupture with Marx, but what united them with Marx (and Nietzsche) was precisely this relativism. Only, Marx still clung to one last vestige of objective truth. He relativized everything save for Marxism, which somehow stood above the historical currents that shaped all other ideas. Those currents, he moreover insisted, would inevitably carry man toward Communism. The postmodernists, however, cast off entirely the fraying ropes that tied Western philosophy to the quest for ultimate truths.

Michel Foucault, for example, framed the whole of Western civilization as a repressive apparatus designed to discipline and control human difference of all kinds, whether sexual, racial, or cognitive. Jean-François Lyotard heralded the demise of all "grand narratives"— not just the ancient but also modern ones such as the Enlightenment and modernity. Even empirical science, he taught, amounted to a sort of performative "language game" that served the needs of power. Judith Butler, the hard-line feminist and "queer theory" pioneer, took aim at the gender binary. People don't inherit gender from nature, she contended. Rather, we perform gender in response to societal expectations. Then there was Jean Baudrillard, the weirdest of them all, who claimed that technological society had "murdered" reality itself and replaced it with a network of "hyperreal" simulacra, virtual realities that were "more real than the real".

As with my previous intellectual phases, I jumped all the way down the rabbit hole: Yes, gender differences, aesthetic standards in art, and universal moral rules were all the products of repressive institutions. The point of politics and activism was no longer to seize the means of economic production but to resist racist and sexist "hegemony" in all its forms, starting with language itself, which subtly and insidiously encrypted oppression and hierarchy.

It didn't occur to me that the postmodern demolition of all truth meant that there was no standard left on which to base these various claims for justice. "Social justice", in this view, involved upholding the claims of any group that stood against the West and white, male "privilege". It was no justice at all. Little wonder why Foucault came to admire Khomeini and Butler cheered the terror groups Hezbollah and Hamas, neither of which was known for humane treatment of women and sexual minorities. Baudrillard, meanwhile, was some sort of Maoist. As with Sartre's embrace of the Soviet Union, all sorts of compromises with political evil were permissible down the road from *Zarathustra*.

* * * * *

Ideas have consequences, and the ones I adopted in college only deepened my sense of alienation and removed the examined life further from my grasp. Not once did I pause in those years to ask: What is the secret to true happiness and freedom, and how does it relate to human nature? Materialist theory, whether of the Marxist or post-Marxist variety, foreclosed such reflection, since it denied the existence of human nature as such and considered the individual to be a victim of impersonal forces, be they language, economics, or history.

A victim by definition is not responsible. My philosophy thus licensed irresponsibility and surrender to the appetites. Which is to say that it fit perfectly on a modern college campus. Unlike in Utah, most everyone at UW seemed to drink to excess, smoke pot, and hook up randomly. The guardrails were missing. At times, I almost felt inadequate in the debauchery department. I suffered from the constant anxiety that somewhere, something was going on—a drunken poker game, a bump-and-grind dance party—and I was missing out.

Only, I married my revelry to highfalutin ideas, a combination that made me appear doubly ludicrous when my blood alcohol level surged north of 0.1%. Many were the mornings when I woke up in a cold sweat, my head throbbing, the stink of stale alcohol and vomit competing for my olfactory attention, nausea assailing my innards. What had I done the previous night?

I follow a band of guys from my dorm as they drift from one house party to another. Hip-hop blares on the speakers. A shot of tequila. A party cup brimming with beer. And another and another and another and another. Standing on a porch somewhere. Smoking cigarettes with a gaggle of sorority girls. Trying, and failing, to impress the ladies with my command of high theory. Stumbling and falling.

Then the vomit stench would remind me: By that point in the evening, I had already expunged the contents of my stomach—"Out with the old, in with the new, bro!"—and could barely stand on my two feet. (Yet I had kept drinking more.) What a pathetic sight I must have been! Oh, how they must have laughed at my expense. It was the mental stab wounds of shame that hurt worst of all, and my memory didn't permit me to forget a single one.

If only I could fall back asleep ...

In those black hours, it did me no good to recall that all moral norms are historically contingent or that resisting Western hegemony is the duty of the subaltern. The Angel

of History offered no relief. Instead I would recite the few
Qur'anic verses I knew. Or, more often, I would pray
to a nondenominational Almighty in the sky, much as I
had done as a child all those years earlier. I prayed to God
to condescend to my depths and wipe away my shame.
Then, once the crisis was past, I would feel a bit silly and
return to my materialist certainties.

CHAPTER SEVEN

BORDERLANDS

In a poem of 1577, Saint Teresa of Ávila wrote of how the "mansion of thy mind" is Almighty God's "dwelling-place". God says he roams the mind's corridors,

> Knocking loud, if e'er I find
> In thy thought a closéd door.

That held true even for me. I had tried to shut, lock, and bolt every entryway to God and banish him from my mind. But I couldn't attend to every nook and cranny. Many a secret door remained open to him, if by a crack. On the doors that I *had* managed to shut, I heard the loud knocks that Saint Teresa wrote about. It would take me some years, though, before I could reckon honestly with the fact that, from time to time, and especially in moments of great shame or degradation, I felt compelled to fling the doors open.

In the meanwhile, taking on adult responsibility as a schoolteacher after graduation did me much good. At the slightest contact with reality, much of the bosh that clouded my mind dissipated, and a clear, crisp new horizon presented itself to me.

* * * * *

As graduation neared, I came across a recruitment flier in my dorm building for an organization called Teach for

America. It described the achievement gap between rich and poor children in the United States in starkly statistical terms. Ninety percent of African American students didn't attain math proficiency by eighth grade. Eighty percent of Latinos couldn't read at grade level by the same age. Fewer than one in ten children of all races growing up in poor areas finished college.

Half a century since Martin Luther King's "I Have a Dream" speech, the American promise of equal opportunity remained unfulfilled for most children born in the wrong zip codes. This, the flier said, was "*the* civil rights challenge of our time". The photo on the flier showed a white guy in a button-down and tie facing a classroom of black children, who all had their hands stretched in the air. They all knew the answer to the teacher's question.

The message was electrifying: *If you wish to end inequality, roll up your sleeves, come to a classroom like this one, and teach for two years.* The vaguely leftish rhetoric and imagery flattered my idealism (the organization's approach to educational reform was, in some ways, deeply conservative). Joining TFA, moreover, promised a new start, in a part of the country that I was otherwise unlikely ever to live in. With no definite plans for the future, I threw my hat in the ring. TFA invited me for an interview and then to deliver a sample lesson, which I naturally devoted to Britain's militant labor movement. I thought it was a disaster. Yet I was accepted, and within weeks, before I even had my degree in hand, I decamped from Seattle to my assigned city of Brownsville, Texas.

Situated on the southernmost tip of the Texas Panhandle, minutes away from the United States–Mexico border in the Rio Grande Valley, Brownsville was (and is) one of the neediest cities in the country. Many of my future students would be the children of Mexican migrant farm workers, who spent only a part of the year in Brownsville before harvest season took them to points north in California and beyond. Others resided permanently in *colonias*, unincorporated shantytowns that lacked potable water and other basic services. Nine out of ten received free or reduced-price school meals courtesy of the federal government. Gang violence, much of it tied to the cross-border drug trade, cast a long shadow over their lives.

After a weeklong orientation to these cheerful realities, TFA sent us to Houston, where it operated one of several summer boot camps for the incoming 2005 corps of teachers. The Houston "institute", as it was called, was a crucible of sweat, tears, and sixteen-hour workdays.

We mustered at six in the morning or earlier and spent the first half of the day teaching summer-school students. Lunchtime brought soggy sandwiches and an all-too-brief respite before the afternoon pedagogy seminars, which packed into a few hours what conventional teachers spent years studying in education school. Evenings were reserved for grading homework and planning the following day's lessons and still more seminars and colloquia. Five hours of restless shut-eye were considered a good night's sleep.

It was an article of faith in TFA that teacher quality is the most decisive factor in good schools. By setting ambitious goals, meticulously planning lessons, and rigidly enforcing classroom discipline, it was possible to deliver educational excellence in America's benighted inner cities. Above all, the organization insisted, great educators "worked relentlessly". To repair the country's "failure factories", it was necessary to adopt the professional habits normally associated with large law firms and high-end consultancies. Hence, the grueling schedule.

The TFA worldview ran counter to the one that prevailed in the teaching profession. The teachers' unions and education schools held that the achievement gap resulted from inadequate funding, parental neglect, rampant poverty, and other "systemic" ills that were beyond educators' control. In this way, the educator's ideology shifted accountability for student learning from teachers to lawmakers, parents, and society at large. And it insinuated that some kids—those from low-income, minority backgrounds—couldn't be held to the same expectations as others.

That view was probably closer to my own. Upon entering the teaching profession, I was sure that the achievement gap was purely a matter of redistributive justice. Children from Brownsville would perform at the same level as those from the wealthy suburbs of Houston, if only they had access to the same material resources. Spreading the wealth from rich to poor would likewise abate the criminality and disorder that blighted the Rio Grande Valley. As a TFA corps member, then, the best I could do was to apply a Band-Aid to a gushing wound that would heal only once society was remade to serve the needs of the many rather than the few.

Still, I was committed to the TFA mission in a general sense. I recalled Marx' famous dictum that "the philosophers have only interpreted the world, in various ways; the point is to change it." My TFA stint, I thought, would bring me to the wretched of the earth, who would be grateful for my solidarity and deep leftist convictions. Only, I considered myself to be above the day-to-day tedium of teacher training. Instead of rolling up my sleeves, I spent much of my time at the institute chasing hookups; the ratio of young women to men in TFA was highly advantageous to the latter. I slipped out for beer during not a few of the afternoon pedagogy sessions.

* * * * *

Then there was the TFA diversity training. Partly to prepare mostly white teachers for work in minority-majority classrooms and partly, I suspect, to defang objections to its no-excuses philosophy from progressive quarters, TFA asked us constantly to "unpack" our identity "privileges". We would reflect in small groups on an irredeemably racist, sexist, classist, and homophobic America, and lament how, by dint of our social advantages, we TFAers had been accomplices to these evils—that is, except for those who belonged to the downtrodden groups.

These self-criticism sessions unfolded according to a certain unwritten script, and most TFAers quickly learned how to play their assigned roles. There was a ladder of oppression, with straight, white men occupying the top steps, white women in the middle, and minorities below them. To get to the most-prized spots, at the bottom, one had to be a member of a racial minority, female, *and* "queer". Add a physical disability to the mix, and you would be crowned king—or rather, queen—of the oppressed.

Those at the top of the ladder were, paradoxically, the losers. They were called to repent. Those closer to the bottom, the winners, were expected to vent grievance. As a "Muslim" immigrant in post-9/11 America, for example, I was supposed to complain about racial profiling at airports. In fact, I had never faced such discrimination, though sometimes, when I sensed that my Iranian background might be an issue in certain social settings, I would preemptively joke that "I come from the heart of the Axis of Evil."

This aspect of the TFA training regimen was distasteful, and I wasn't alone in thinking so. One of the most outspoken members was Yossi, a twenty-two-year-old Israeli American who had joined TFA from the University of Pennsylvania. English wasn't Yossi's first language, yet he spoke it eloquently, albeit with a heavy Israeli accent. Yossi was not a child of privilege. He had hustled to put himself through the Ivy League. According to the script, however, he was supposed to self-flagellate.

"You can't stuff people into these little boxes!" Yossi fumed in these diversity sessions. His voice squeaked, and he punctuated his comments with wild hand gestures, which instantly recalled the region of the world we both hailed from.

To my own amazement, I found myself nodding in agreement with his "reactionary" opinions, and even adding my voice to his: "Yeah, in the grand scheme of things, this country is pretty tolerant!"

Yossi and I became pals. Ours was one of those fiery friendships that are characterized by intense rivalry and true comradeship and regular cycles of enmity and reconciliation. And though it didn't outlast our time in TFA, in my case the friendship proved to be a providential source of grace and a spur toward my ultimate conversion.

The poor TFA diversity coach, who had only recently completed her own stint, was flustered when we veered off-script: "Folks, I think we should all, like, acknowledge that, even if we don't immediately recognize it, most of us have, like, been taking advantage of privilege? So, if I could ask folks to ground ourselves around issues of personal experience instead of, like, making general statements?" (This style of "up-speak", in which declarative sentences took an interrogative inflection, spread among TFAers like a viral contagion of unknown origin.)

I knew that identity politics had trickled down to TFA from the intellectual world that I inhabited. It was Marx who had reduced all history, and all values, to the war of group against group. Later, the postmodern theory of "intersectionality" claimed to lay bare the hidden "structures of oppression" that subjugated minorities along overlapping lines of race, gender, and sexuality.

Put into practice—minus the revolutionary bits in Marxism, of course—these ideas looked something like a TFA diversity session, where it was forbidden to talk of anything common to all people, anything that transcended race-gender-sex dynamics. Every "general statement"— that is, every universalist truth claim—was an imposition of power. It was one's race, gender, sexual orientation, and class that determined one's opinions about nearly everything that mattered. Everyone was partial, but some people's partiality counted more than others'.

But that was ridiculous and, more important, utterly discordant with my experience. What, really, did I have to complain about? I might have written about "capitalist hegemony" in an abstract sense. But the "Oppressed Immigrant" role simply didn't fit me. I didn't feel like a victim. I was beginning to learn, in other words, that life itself could supply the best gauge for measuring political claims, provided one was honest enough with oneself.

* * * * *

It happened that Yossi and I were to teach at the same middle school in Brownsville. When training was over, and we returned to the Valley, the two of us moved into a roomy bungalow together with a couple of other TFA members. Yossi, who had majored in English, was hired to teach the same subject to sixth graders. Without giving it much thought, I had checked a box on my TFA application indicating that I wished to work with children with disabilities, and the school took me up on the offer.

I knew nothing about how to help kids with autism, dyslexia, behavioral disorders, and the like. What I lacked in expertise, however, I made up for with a carpetbagger's smugness and braggadocio. It didn't help that the school administration treated the new TFA hires, at least initially, as if we were the Valley's last, best hope. That in turn only kindled resentment among the local teachers, some of whom really knew what they were doing.

Yossi could be prone to similar snobbery. Yet he also spent nearly every waking hour making sure that his kids could read and write at or above grade level. He would get to his class before dawn and stay long after the final bell; there weren't enough hours during the regular day for all the assessing, grading, mentoring, and lesson planning that he felt he needed to do. When he returned home late at night, his clothes would be soaked with sweat. He wouldn't come out for drinks but on the rarest of occasions, no matter how much the rest of us cajoled him.

The same couldn't be said for me. My main job was to run a "resource center", basically a holding area for students who were disabled or otherwise disruptive. When I first took over the center, I festooned its walls with posters of Muhammad Ali, Malcolm X, Cesar Chavez, and other 1960s and '70s political icons, whom I assumed my students would reverence. I introduced myself to the kids as "Mr. A"—"as in, the grades you're going to earn!"—and talked about our "big goals" and the "relentless pursuit of knowledge".

Such ardor was necessary but not sufficient. Running the resource center effectively also required close collaboration with the regular-education teachers, and I quickly despaired at the enormity of the problem. In any given period, a dozen kids would pour into my room in haphazard fashion, each requiring assistance with a different subject: Daniel, who suffered from dyslexia, had to get through a chapter in a young-adult novel; Maricela, with Down syndrome, needed to create a timeline of Civil War battles; hot-tempered Jose needed to cool off; and so on.

Usually my aides and I ended up doing the work for them. This defeated the true purpose of special education, which was to help students with disabilities master the same knowledge and skills as the other students, albeit in modified form. What was the point? When the final bell rang, I drove straight home, having left my students no worse—and no better off—than they would have been without me. I spent much of the first year of my stint going out to bars and dating a succession of fellow TFAers. The longest of these relationships would last four years.

I figured out that I could maintain the esteem of the administrators by making an outward showing of professionalism and talking a big game in faculty meetings. As far as the school leadership was concerned, I was a star. It was Yossi who found himself in hot water, over his refusal to grade generously. Instead of automatically passing failing students, he insisted that they come to him after school for extra instruction. That didn't make him popular among parents or the principals, and at one point he came close to being fired.

"Dude, don't you want to get to Harvard Law after this?" I would ask him. "Wouldn't it look bad if you had to disclose being fired from your TFA gig?"

"I wasn't brought here to hand out grades like candy," he replied. His voice squeaked more than usual. "They haven't learned. When they learn, I will pass them."

"OK, but why not ease up *a bit*?"

"Because. Then I'd be lying."

In the moment, all I could muster was a smirk, as if to say: OK, buddy. If you want to commit career suicide, suit yourself.

Weeks and months passed by. Yossi was not fired. He stood his ground. In the end, it was the school administration that bent to his will, rather than the other way around.

By then I was utterly in awe of my roommate. It really was the case that, even in the direst classrooms, teachers could make tremendous gains with students by emphasizing hard work, honesty, and tough discipline. But there was much more to it than that. Yossi's refusal to countenance a lie—no matter how troublesome the truth—marked a milestone in my moral education.

I resolved to pour myself into my job. I didn't manage to keep the resolution every day. Indeed, I failed more often than not. But even the thought, as well as the attendant anguish when I fell short of my daily vows, were new for me. All this may not sound like an earthshaking realization, but it was for me. It suggested that there were gradations of character in all human circumstances. That there was great value in old moralistic notions I used to sneer at. And, maybe, that there were permanent things about what made all people tick.

* * * * *

The intellectual consequences were far-reaching. When it came to education reform, for starters, it was clear to me that, contrary to my original assumption, no amount of redistributive justice could make a difference without good teaching, which, in the final analysis, had little to do with small class sizes, a laptop for every student, more opportunities for creative expression, or any of the other proposals typically floated by progressives.

Rather, good teaching was at heart about *order*—order, in the teacher's mind, about the lesson he was going to impart on a given day; order in the minds of students, who needed routine, regularity, and predictability from adults; and order in the sense that peace reigned in the classroom and those who disturbed it knew what to expect. I witnessed this firsthand, because my duties required me to follow the same cohort of special-education students to their regular-education classrooms. I could thus observe how they fared with different teachers.

Mrs. X, an eighth-grade math teacher, spent much of her time browsing the web and often relied on dull worksheets to keep her students busy. Her room was a chaos of crumpled paper and flying spitballs. "Come on, guys, settle down," she would lamely moan, but the kids mostly ignored her—until she lost her temper and hollered at them. Her overreaction, however, further undercut her authority, and a few minutes later the spitballs went flying again.

Yossi, on the other hand, greeted each student at the door with a firm handshake. He delivered rich lessons and never compromised on his disciplinary rules. Every infraction was met with a "demerit", every good deed with a "merit", and there was an escalating chain of negative and positive consequences associated with each. The kids loved him because he supplied the structure and stability that were missing from their homes.

You could have installed the latest technology in Mrs. X's room, reduced her class size, given her all the extra time she needed for planning and professional development, and so forth, yet her students still wouldn't learn much. Conversely, you could have shut off the electricity to Yossi's room and forced him to teach by candlelight, doubled his class size, taken away his computer and planning hour, and chances were, he still would have managed to work educational wonders.

Character and virtue, then, preceded material circumstances; leftist ideology put the cart before the horse. People and their conduct weren't reducible to language, race, class, and collective identities. There was something more in the virtuous—a capacity to recognize the good and a desire to spread it around them, to bring order where disorder prevailed. The kids grasped the passion for order in teachers like Yossi, and they reacted accordingly. Indeed, you could have teleported his classroom to a country in, say, East Asia, and an unbiased observer, even one who spoke a different language, would have felt compelled to say: "That teacher is pursuing order and excellence."

The lesson held true across life's various realms. In TFA circles, Yossi had a reputation for honesty and constancy. He was a trustworthy friend, to whom one could turn in happiness or distress. By contrast, I probably came across as selfish, aloof, imperious. It may have been fun to shoot the philosophical breeze with me over a bottle of wine, but no one would say of me: "Here's a man you can rely on."

When I subjected myself to interior scrutiny, as I was beginning to do, I had to admit that the impression reflected an underlying truth. These character contrasts, in turn, implied the existence of a universal standard of good conduct, an objective morality. In my case, awareness of that universal standard first arose, not from any external source, but from a voice—more often a whisper—inside.

Well, where did that that voice or whisper originate? And was it a coincidence that my former worldview— the one that said that morality is merely a function of power, history, biology, language—gave me an alibi for shutting out the whisper when its remonstrances became inconvenient? In time, the search for answers to these two questions would force me to think deeply about the phenomenon of conscience. The voice inside that urged me to do good and shun evil, I would conclude, gave unimpeachable testimony to the existence of a personal God. But not yet.

* * * * *

For now, it was enough that my time in Teach for America disabused me of my leftist certainties and turned my worldview upside down—or rather, right side up.

Yossi played no small part in my political volte-face. Early on, he and I locked horns over matters geopolitical. Our countries of birth—Iran and Israel—were Mideast archenemies, and their tensions spilled over into our friendship. The Iraq War was frequently the immediate focus of these quarrels. Like any good leftist, I took it for granted that America had invaded Iraq to plunder the country's oil. I was sure, too, that Israel's malign influence in Washington had something to do with the decision.

Once, toward the beginning of our stint, we nearly came to blows over these questions. Yossi was no great fan of the war. His point, however, was that the facts didn't bear out my conspiracy narrative. Perhaps Operation Iraqi Freedom had been a mistake, he granted. Yet President Bush had based his decision on the best intelligence that was available at the time—namely, that Saddam Hussein, a tyrant who had long destabilized the region, was bent on developing weapons of mass destruction.

"But there were no WMD!" I yelled.

"Correct," Yossi replied, his squeaking more pronounced than ever. "But every Western intelligence agency thought there was."

"Yeah, right! If by 'every intelligence agency', you mean the Mossad!"

The hard Left has long had a penchant for slandering and pouring opprobrium on the Jewish state while whitewashing or ignoring the far-worse crimes of anti-Western and anti-Israel regimes. I was not immune to this tendency. I had dropped the Iranian, Islamic style of Israel obsession only to pick up the *New Left Review* variety.

At this, Yossi lost it: "You anti-Semitic piece of garbage!"

It took the intervention of our other roommates to prevent the debate from getting physical.

Yossi and I buried the hatchet a few days later, after I did a bit of research and discovered that the Mossad had *not* urged an invasion of Iraq, while most major Western intelligence agencies had indeed concurred in the judgment that Saddam was developing WMD. The blunder was both an embarrassment and a wake-up call. Being educated and holding "progressive" opinions was no guarantee against prejudice, especially when the prejudice arose from the ideological air I breathed. Afterward I developed a lifelong intellectual antibody against all manner of conspiratorial thinking, especially the kind, all too common among people from the Middle East, that singles out Jews and the Jewish state as the source of the world's troubles.

The ugly scene became a blessing in disguise in another way, as well. Confronted with evidence of my own prejudice, I was forced finally to study the real history of Marxism and totalitarianism. What else had I gotten wrong? Hitherto, I had uncritically swallowed the line that Marxism was nothing like other violent mass movements. Marxism, according to this view, was a noble and universalist enterprise that sought the liberation of all mankind, regardless of nationality, race, or religion. There might have been some "excesses", yes, but the doctrine couldn't be blamed for its misapplication here and there.

Except, I was increasingly racked with doubt over these assertions. Had I given them sufficient critical thought? Had I read any reliable books, anything other than standard-issue Marxist apologetics? The answer was no, on both counts. I had to rectify my ignorance.

I immersed myself in the website of Yad Vashem, Israel's official Holocaust memorial, and shed copious tears over the evils visited upon the Jews of Europe and over the "Righteous Gentiles" who had risked their lives to rescue them. At the same time, I opened my library, and my mind, to books by survivors and critics of Communist totalitarianism, among them Václav Havel, Arthur Koestler, George Orwell, and Natan Sharansky. I read a thorough history of modern China, which detailed the horrors of the Great Leap Forward and the Cultural Revolution.

Whether they called themselves Communist or National Socialist, modern totalitarians were kindred spirits, united by the faith that man was infinitely malleable. Once people acceded to that premise, they could abide any crime—be it the extermination of six million Jews, man-made famine in Ukraine, or the terrorist depredations of Islamist movements. The slogans differed, but the real-world results were all too similar.

I now shuddered at ideas that I had entertained a few months earlier. I wanted nothing more to do with man-made utopias of any kind. In fact, I wanted to rededicate my life to thwarting the utopians. I became a conservative almost instantly, though I didn't embrace that label right away.

* * * * *

Koestler's anti-Communist masterpiece *Darkness at Noon* (1941) was a particularly formative influence. It offered both a piercing diagnosis of the totalitarian tendency and an intellectual and spiritual blueprint for resisting it. The Hungarian-born British writer, himself an ex-Marxist, presented a thinly novelized account of the Stalinist show trials of the 1930s. The victims of the trials had been former revolutionaries, many of them from the founding generation of Bolshevism, who had fallen out of favor with the party.

The novel's protagonist, Nicholas Rubashov, is one such figure, a veteran apparatchik, who, in his own heyday, hadn't hesitated to ruin others if the party required it.

Now Rubashov has outlived his usefulness to "that mocking oracle they called history". Arrested in the dead of
night, he is targeted for "physical liquidation". Yet Stalinism's twisted logic requires that its victims fess up to a slate
of elaborate trumped-up charges before they can be put to
death. Will he submit to one last lie for the party's sake?

Rubashov's trouble is that, after a lifetime of service to
Communism, he still clings to thin remnants of his conscience. In prison, the ghosts of those he has destroyed
haunt him. Nor can he let go of a certain "grammatical
fiction"—the first-person perspective—which is to say, of
individuality and personhood. But his interrogators have
no such scruples. They believe that they "are tearing the
old skin off mankind and giving it a new one", as one of
them puts it. Their deadly, godless cult justifies all means
for obtaining secular salvation.

Rubashov himself had once been a high priest in that
religion. But now, sleep-deprived under torture and
nearly delirious, he thinks back to a certain *Pietà*, a scene
of the Blessed Virgin holding the dead body of her Son.
Rubashov had run across the *Pietà* when he was still in
good standing with the party, but he had never paused to
study it. The memory of it now reminds him that "perhaps
it did not suit man to be completely freed from old bonds,
from the steadying brakes of 'Thou shalt not.' " As his ren-
dezvous with the dialectic comes to an end, the hardened
Communist pays tribute to the Ten Commandments—
and to the Cross.

A single novel—a single sentence!—unlocked a great
truth for me. Man needed the "steadying brakes" of God's
laws and the sacrifice of One who stands in for all of history's victims and perpetrators. The old "thou shalts" and the
heartbreaking sacrifice that I read about in Saint Matthew's
Gospel were a bulwark against totalitarianism, perhaps the

only durable ones. The God who revealed himself in the moral law, and who condescended to be scourged and crucified by his creation—this God was a liberator.

To restrain man's hand against man, he had to be bound by some absolute authority outside himself. Unbounded by such an Absolute Other, man would follow the siren song of political evil and use any means in pursuit of political ends. It was wrong to think that belief in God was impossible after Auschwitz; rather, Auschwitz was possible *because* God had been pronounced dead and all the old "thou shalts" declared null and void.

The democratic West started from different premises— namely, that the human person is rights-bearing and possessed of an inherent dignity that rulers couldn't transgress. I had lived long enough in Iran and the United States to tell the difference. Six or seven years earlier, I had been under the ayatollahs' thumb. Now *that* was real oppression. The United States had welcomed me, and in a short time I had gone from a trailer park to an elite teacher corps. In between, I had backed a political movement that was dedicated to overthrowing America's economic system, albeit nonviolently.

What would have happened to me had I flirted with an outfit like Worker's Alliance under the Islamic Republic? No doubt, I would have had my fingernails pulled out somewhere in the bowels of Tehran's Evin Prison.

Well, why was the West different? How was it possible to uphold the dignity of the person if there wasn't something special about his origins? Why should rulers feel constrained in their power? It seemed to me that, to the extent that Western democracies were morally superior, it was in large part because they still hewed to a Judeo- Christian line, however faded. In this sense Nietzsche had been right: Egalitarian democracy was a product, or an extension, of biblical religion, and that was a *good* thing. The real peril was that Western democracy would detach itself from its religious underpinnings. The flower thus uprooted would wilt.

* * * * *

These were for the most part intuitive and rudimentary conclusions. I still had only the vaguest notions of what "biblical religion" stood for, in itself and as a wellspring of political truth. But my intuitions were fundamentally sound, and the more philosophy and history that I read, the more convinced I became that the West's humane, free civilization couldn't be understood, or sustained, outside the spiritual soil that had nurtured it. If I savored the ordered liberty that I saw around me, I had to give credit to the religious ideals that had given birth to it.

Appreciating the Judeo-Christian foundations of the West didn't make me a Christian, of course. But it helped. Thereafter, when I was asked about my religious views, I no longer bragged about my atheism. Instead, I would say: "I'm not fortunate enough to be a person of faith." The knocks on the doors of my mind sounded louder by the day.

CHAPTER EIGHT

THREE FEASTS

Like most of the world's great cities, New York can read your mind and magnify your mood. There is nothing supernatural at work in this. If you are feeling up, you will take in the gorgeous urban vistas, the chic bars with their well-dressed patrons, the neo-Gothic churches and handsome prewar buildings nestled among glass high-rises that shimmer under the sapphire sky pierced by sunlight. Manhattan will answer your joy with its own.

But if you are down, you notice, instead, those garbage bags piled high at the street corner, that canine-sized rat scurrying on the subway track, the aggressive vendor hawking homemade rap CDs and garish T-shirts, and much else of the kind. The people crowding the sidewalks— smart-looking Wall Street guys, panhandlers and druggies, tourists and fashionistas—appear coldly indifferent if not outright hostile. A heavy rain then strikes the psychological coup de grâce.

It was in this latter state of Manhattan dejection that I found myself one Sunday afternoon in the spring of 2008. I was twenty-three at the time. Having finished my Teach for America stint in Texas, I had followed a TFA girlfriend to her home state of Massachusetts and was teaching at a charter school in Salem, about an hour's drive northeast of Boston. To earn extra money, I worked for TFA on the side, helping train the new recruits at the New York City institute.

That night I was due to return home after a TFA working weekend in New York—one of my first visits to the city that I would later call home—but there were hours to kill before my train out of the city departed Penn Station. In the interval, I circled a four-block radius around the station over and over, trying in vain to shake a crushing hangover while my mind's eye replayed scenes from the ruinous weekend.

* * * * *

The First Feast

It started with a Friday happy hour in Salem. I was supposed to drive to Boston to catch the Acela to New York after school, but I couldn't say no to a drink. "Just one beer," I thought. I downed two. A boozy warmth surged inside me when I sat behind the wheel. I turned the volume dial on the stereo to full blast. The car vibrated to the repetitive *thump-thump-thump* of techno music, and I couldn't hear a thing outside as I pulled away. Time seemed to speed up.

Traffic was mild, and I knew my way around the area's labyrinthine roads. I was tapping the steering wheel and nodding my head to the rhythm when I came to the stoplight that divided Salem from the next town over. The light turned green. I pressed the accelerator. The next thing I knew, a car zooming in the other direction was right in front of me. Brakes screamed. Metal slammed into metal. Broken bits of headlight glass flew into the air. The two cars turned a half circle, dancing a tango in the middle of the intersection before they came to a screeching halt.

The collision and the accompanying adrenaline rush snapped my mind back to reality. My speakers were still blasting sound and air. *Thump-thump-thump.* My first cogent thought was that the right of way had been mine. I seized on it immediately and began repeating the words to myself like a mantra: "I had the right of way! I had the right of way!"

Only, there was something peculiar about the other car. It was a Ford Interceptor, painted navy blue and white. There were coruscating red lights on the roof, and large letters on the sides read: POLICE. Then I recalled that I was still driving on my Texas license and didn't have car insurance (the latter was a misdemeanor criminal offense in Massachusetts). Like my father with his conscription, I couldn't be bothered with a day's worth of paperwork to renew my lapsed insurance and obtain a Massachusetts driver's license.

"What's your malfunction, huh?" the burly officer asked once we stepped out to survey the damage. I had carved a sizable dent into the passenger-side door of his Interceptor, totaling the front of my Camry in the process.

"I'm so, so sorry, sir! I could have sworn my light was green."

"I was in pursuit, you moron! You're supposed to yield!"

Ah, I would have heard his sirens wailing but for the *thump-thump-thump* of the techno. I called my girlfriend and told her that I had "messed up—bad. Really bad this time." She was welcome to leave me forever, I said, because no one should have to stay with someone as useless at life as I was. I imagined I would be booked for driving under the influence, the officer would sue me for whip-lash injury, and, without insurance, I would be forced to declare bankruptcy. My life was over before it had begun. I prayed to my nondenominational deity.

In the event, the officer let me off with a warning for failure to yield to an emergency vehicle. He didn't make me take a breath analyzer test or even require me to show proof of insurance, though I would later have to pay the police department for the damage to his car. Had he been a stickler for procedure, my life might have taken an entirely different course from that day. Maybe it was the luck of fools and young people. Or was it the prayer?

* * * * *

The Second Feast

When I got to New York the next day, I dove right back into drunken debauchery. My excuse was that I needed to soothe my accident-rankled nerves, and the frat-bro types among the TFA staff all agreed that a long, healing bender was in order. After the day's working sessions, we ventured out to McSorley's, the old Irish redoubt in the East Village. Time sped up once more as we emptied pint after pint of the pub's signature light and dark ales. A drunken stranger poured a whole pint on my suit at one point. The feast, my second of the weekend, went on.

I got back to my hotel room at three in the morning. Sunday's session was due to start at seven. I woke up in a panic at half past, threw up the previous night's beer-and-Irish-cheddar medley, and raced to the TFA offices. The rest of the day went about as well as it had begun. My emetic exertions colored my eyes a demonic crimson. The stink of beery sweat wafted from my body. My head felt as if an invisible crew of Lilliputian workers had descended upon it to complete a construction project that for some reason entailed drilling a thousand tiny holes into my brain.

Worst, I feared that every one of my colleagues, even the ones who hadn't come out with us, had somehow been privy to the previous night's revelry. They had *all* heard my every vulgar joke, watched in revulsion as I shoved cheese down my gullet like a wild man, and observed my drunken attempts to pick up girls while supposedly in a relationship. My mind transmogrified my bad conscience into paranoia. I felt exposed, though I was fully clothed.

Throughout the session, the point of which was to train us to train new teachers, I avoided wading into the discussions as much as possible. Yet I felt obliged not to stay mute the whole time, so I would occasionally blurt out some remarks to make it appear that I was paying attention. In fact, all I could think about were the Lilliputians with their drills and jackhammers, and my words sounded to me like so much ill-considered gibberish. At one point, I unaccountably burst out in hysterical laughter mid-remark.

These interventions invariably elicited awkward silences from the working group, forcing the director of the institute to "transition us back to the question at hand", as he would put it. At the end of the day I approached the director, intending to say ... what? I wasn't even sure when I sought him out. He was another straitlaced Ivy Leaguer, a hyperprofessional, sober, thoroughly humorless.

"I know I didn't live up to my, er, fullest potential today ..."

"Oh?" he answered, coyly raising an eyebrow, as if to suggest that he had no idea what I was talking about.

"Yes, well, you know, I couldn't help thinking that some of the stuff you said was really coded criticism directed at me."

He denied it.

What I wanted to say—to yell at the top of my lungs, really—was: "I know I sounded and acted like a besotted donkey. That's not what I'm normally like. I'll do better next time." Instead, I came across as vaguely adversarial, as if he were somehow to blame for my disastrous day, for not sufficiently accommodating my hangover. After a pause, he reassured me that he had every expectation that I would achieve great things as a school leader at the New York institute. "Go home and get some rest."

His response was infuriatingly cheery. Now I realized why I had asked him for a meeting in the first place. I wanted him to tell me how lousy my performance had been. I wanted to be judged and condemned. Perhaps at some level I even wanted him to fire me. Instead, all I got was a minor motivational boost. We left it at that.

* * * * *

The Third Feast

So it was that I ended up circling around Penn Station that Sunday afternoon while waiting for my train to depart for Boston. My mind kept conjuring images from the previous weekend like some confounded looping slideshow: the beers in Salem; my front bumper crushing into the side of a police car; the night of excess in the Village; Sunday's humiliation.

"When are you going to change?" I kept asking myself.

In one sense, I had already changed. I had given up my college radicalism. I had learned that character and morality both trump and determine the order of material things, rather than the other way around. I had made peace with American society and learned to appreciate the very aspects of it that I used to disdain the most. But I was not at peace with myself.

This interior unease manifested itself most acutely in my penchant for strong drink. I wasn't a chronic heavy drinker. I could go weeks and months without touching a bottle. But when I drank, *I drank.* One of the worst of these episodes had occurred during an earlier visit to New York, around Christmastime in 2006, when, already sloshed, I decided that it would be a good idea to buy a baggie of cocaine from a street dealer and unleash my inner Tony Montana. Fortunately, my first coke trip so terrified me that I never touched the white stuff again.

My life had been on an upward trajectory ever since I graduated from college. I had adopted the Yossi/TFA work ethic as my own, and no one who knew me would deny that I was driven and ambitious. But there were these occasional bursts of self-destructive behavior. Too often I found myself apologizing to friends and colleagues for "what I said last night" or for "how I acted over drinks". Shame begat shame, and the cycle repeated itself, even as I went from worldly success to success.

I thought I was sufficiently rooted in myself to live wisely, that my personal code supplied what others found in the moral precepts of religious faith. Yet as the weekend of disaster had shown, my code could be as flexible as a jellyfish in the face of my appetites. Nor did it offer much by way of consolation once those appetites led me astray. I couldn't break the cycle of transgression and shame on my own. *When are you going to change?*

These thoughts pinballed about my mind as I walked in circles in New York that afternoon. My dazed path took me repeatedly by a Capuchin monastery located around the block from Penn Station. The building had a nondescript brick facade. It wasn't obvious that it housed a church and monastic order but for the relief above the entrance, of an almost alien-looking Jesus, his slender body draped in a long formless robe, arms outstretched to embrace the city. On the third or fourth go-around, I went inside.

It was the first time that I had visited a place of worship on my own accord, as an adult. The Sunday evening Mass was about to begin.

At that point, I had a faint idea that Catholicism was the "original form" of Christianity, which to my mind heightened its prestige. I also had some familiarity, via my mother, with the Church's sacred-art tradition. I had watched *The Godfather*, with its famous Baptism scene intercut with flashes of mob murder. These superficial cultural associations represented the sum total of my knowledge of the faith. What mattered was that I was hungry for God, and in his infinite mercy our Lord pointed me to his Eucharistic presence.

The first thing I noticed on entering the vestibule was the serenity of the place, which struck me as almost impossible, miraculous even, amid the pandemonium of Midtown. As Catholic churches go, the inside wasn't exactly impressive. Or anyway, I don't remember being dazzled by the icons and altars. I parked myself somewhere in the back, and I would remain seated the whole time. When the parishioners stood up, I didn't move. When they knelt, I stayed put. When they prayed, I kept silent. I was only peripherally aware of what the friar was up to at the altar.

Even at that moment, with my deep spiritual longing, there was a part of me that scoffed at the sacred mysteries. While a young guy with an acoustic guitar and a manbun led the parishioners in singing various hymns, the thought that crossed my mind was: You're too smart for this. What if someone I knew spotted me? Then I would forever be counted among the ranks of these gullible saps. But all of a sudden, the singing and strumming dissolved into that all-encompassing serenity, and something extraordinary happened.

"On the night he was betrayed," said the friar, "he took bread and gave thanks and praise. He broke the bread, and gave it to his disciples, saying, 'Take this, all of you, and eat it, for this is my body which will be given up for you.'"

Then he held up with both hands a little white disk (I didn't know it was bread), a bell rang out thrice, and I felt waves of peace wash over me. I was as still as a statue. Tears streamed from my eyes and down my face. These were tears neither of sadness nor even of happiness. They were tears of peace.

The friar continued: "When supper was ended, he took the cup. Again he gave you thanks and praise, gave the cup to his disciples, and said: 'Take this, all of you, and drink from it: This is the cup of my blood, the blood of the new and everlasting covenant. It will be shed for you and for all so that sins may be forgiven. Do this in memory of me.'"

Now the friar held up a golden cup. The bell rang thrice more. My silent tears gave way to choked sobs. I was in the proximity of an awesome and mysterious force—a force bound up with sacrifice, with self-giving unto death, the idea that had made my heart tremble ever since I was a boy. I was aware, too, of my own abjection and smallness, which made me think that I didn't belong in the presence of this holy thing. Not sixteen hours earlier, I had drunk myself into a stupor. I had willingly degraded myself. Now I dared to show up here? And yet, peace continued to radiate from the altar and from the friar's words and hands. I covered my face and bent over in my pew. I did not kneel.

I wept still more as the parishioners took Communion, and the Mass came to an end. I made sure I was the last to leave and managed to compose myself before I got to the vestibule, where the friar was standing to greet the exiting parishioners. I shook his hand and even managed to produce a smile. But before stepping out into the street, I went up to the little portrait of Pope Benedict XVI that hung nearby. The German pontiff was waving warmly in the picture, presumably at an adoring crowd in Saint Peter's Square. The image sent me into another rapture of tears. Once more, I was choking back sobs and struggling to catch my breath.

The friar, who had witnessed all this, came up to me and asked if I was OK.

I mumbled something incoherent.

"That's the pope, you see," the friar said.

I was slightly annoyed at this even in the midst of my emotional outpouring. "I'm not *that* ignorant, old man!" I said to myself. But all I could muster in response was a yes followed by another incoherent, teary mumble.

The friar was undeterred: "That's not God, son. You see, that man's the pope. But he's not God."

Of course, I knew that the pope wasn't God! But then why had his picture brought tears to my eyes? It wasn't so much who Benedict was—I had yet to read any of his writings—as what he stood for. For a twenty-three-year-old groping his way through the mess of modern life, and the mess he had made of his own life, Pope Benedict XVI stood for the principle of continuous, even absolute, authority—the authority of the Roman Catholic Church, in other words, which the pope embodied, and which shone through his portrait. I longed for stable authority as well as redemption. But I was too overpowered in the moment to communicate any of this lucidly. I said a muffled good-bye to the friar and left his church.

CHAPTER NINE

ET INCARNATUS EST

On at least one other occasion, I went to Mass following a bout of heavy drinking that filled me with shame and self-disgust. After these encounters with the Mass, I could no longer truthfully describe myself as an atheist. My emotions and, more important, my imagination had partially assented to faith. Yet my reason and intellect refused to go along. In public, I continued to profess atheism for a few more years still. Like a beloved pair of shoes, my "not fortunate to be a believer" boilerplate was worn out, and I refused to discard it.

Until one day, I did.

* * * * *

At no point did I consider taking up the religion that the accident of birth had assigned me. The Islamic Republic had ruined Islam for me, and the argument that radical Islamism was a gross distortion of an otherwise peaceful and reasonable faith never persuaded me. It was, in truth, little more than a polite myth. I knew well my Iranian history, and I knew that the Arabs had converted the Persian Empire at the edge of the sword, not through interfaith dialogue. Islam was much more than a Hejazi cult of conquest, to be sure, but it was that, too.

When I thought about Islam, then, I did so mainly in political terms. Like all millennial Americans, I had come of age in the shadow of the 9/11 attacks. But I carried an additional burden of memory and anxiety that I had brought over from the old country. Every time I read about an Islamist bombing somewhere, or about Western cartoonists and filmmakers assassinated by men crying "Allahu Akbar", I felt Khomeini's stern glare on my back.

I had already lost one country because totalitarianism and violent revolution—"the red and the black" (Communism and Islamism), as the last shah of Iran had described his enemies—had put millions under their spell. I did not want to lose America, which had given me refuge and treated me with such forbearance and generosity, to these same forces. Married to modern totalitarian methods and ideology, I knew, Islam could imperil a Western civilization that I had come to adore as an orphan adores his adoptive parents.

In 2009, I quit teaching after four years and enrolled at the Northeastern University School of Law in Boston, ostensibly because I wanted to practice a remunerative profession. Intellectually, however, I was much more interested in answering the big questions—about Islam, democracy, and the West—than I was in the nitty-gritty of civil procedure, torts, and contracts. While still in law school, I launched a personal weblog, where I riffed on these themes. I dreamt of breaking into newspapers and magazines.

My immediate concern was the alienated, separatist mindset that prevailed among Muslims residing within the West's frontiers. The solution was assimilation. The United States, I thought, should never tolerate parallel communities like those that ringed many European cities, where Shariah norms trumped secular law and civil authorities hesitated to tread. Yet, early on, I was convinced that liberalism (in the classical sense) could absorb

the Islamic challenge, provided the law was enforced uni-
formly and new arrivals pressed to adopt Western ways.

Later I would have second thoughts about this. A skeptical and infertile West lacked the spiritual resources to
deal with an energetic and virile Islam. Something more
was called for. To deal humanely and intelligently with
Islam within the West, Americans and Europeans needed
to honor their own Judeo-Christian roots—without, of
course, discriminating against the Muslims in their midst.
Such recognition was needed to restore a measure of balance and clarity to the fraught encounter between Islam
and the West.

As for the Middle East, my working theory was that
the region's various venal monarchies and secular autocrats
threatened Western security, either directly (by exporting
Islamic fundamentalism, underwriting terror, and so on)
or indirectly (by misruling their own populations and cre-
ating a vast pool of potential terrorist recruits). I loudly
hailed the Arab Spring uprisings, because I thought that by
promoting democracy across the region, the United States
could safeguard democracy in the West.

In a few short years, I would repent of this theory,
too—or, at least, of a blindly universalist application of
it that didn't pay heed to the cultural and religious threads
that formed the warp and weft of Muslim societies. It was
one thing to take issue with isolationism of the left- and
right-wing varieties; it was quite another to imagine that
toppling strongmen, willy-nilly, would bring freedom to
societies steeped in Islam and tribalism. I should have
known better than to fall for another materialist abstrac-
tion that put the political cart before the moral and cultural horse.

I was on a surer footing when it came to my native land.
Unlike the various Arab kleptocracies, the Iranian regime

was an ideological project in the mold of the Soviet Union and Communist China. It lorded over a people with a rich, pre-Islamic history, a coherent national identity, and a complicated legacy of constitutionalism. Iran was a bigger threat—because it had revanchist designs on the region and saw itself as an ideological rival to the West—and more likely to produce a decent order if and when the present regime collapsed.

Iran's failed Green Revolution gave me my first chance to reach a wider public than my blog's tiny readership. In June 2009, in the summer before I was to start law school, Iranians headed to the polls for a presidential vote. In Iran, unelected bodies vet all candidates for ideological reliability. Most names never make it to the ballot. Even so, the country's educated middle classes—my people—put their hopes that summer in a pair of presidential candidates who promised to ease pervasive repression and give citizens a greater voice.

Voter participation broke records, and the reformists had all the enthusiasm. When the Holocaust-denying, hardline incumbent, Mahmoud Ahmadinejad, claimed victory hours after polls closed, the people had good reason to suspect fraud. Donning green headbands and waving green flags—green being the color of Shiite martyrdom—they poured into the streets by the millions. Their slogan, initially, was "Where Is My Vote?" But within days calls for the overthrow of the regime rang out from Tehran and other major cities. At one point, it seemed as if the Old Colonel's prophecy—that the Islamic Republic would be relegated to the dustbin of history before I finished my education abroad—was about to come true.

It wasn't to be. The Islamic Revolutionary Guard Corps, the regime's praetorians, and the paramilitary *basij* forces cracked down brutally. They sniped at random protesters and charged trucks and motorcycles into defense-less crowds. Arrested activists were taken to makeshift tor-ture camps, where they were raped using batons and soda bottles. The two reform candidates were placed under house arrest, where they languish to this day.

* * * * *

I was despondent, though my grief was of an abstract variety. A decade in the diaspora had strained my heart's ties to Iran, which weren't aortic to begin with. Rather, my support for the Green Movement was an act of faith in Western ideals that I had now fully made my own. Iran in 2009 was a proving ground for those ideals, and it had turned out that an inchoate, sentimental liberalism couldn't overcome an Islamist regime bent on perpetuat-ing itself at any price.

There was a silver lining, however. At the height of the movement, I managed to publish several pieces in prom-inent outlets, including a hoary op-ed in the *Boston Globe* that urged U.S. civil rights activists and labor unions to side with the protesters. Before long I was placing pieces on a wide range of topics in the *Wall Street Journal* and magazines such as the *Weekly Standard*, the *Chronicle of Higher Education*, *Dissent*, and *Commentary*.

At my progressive law school, I won notoriety as some sort of "neocon". I took it as a compliment. The original neoconservatives' journey, from the radical fringes in the 1930s to the American mainstream by the '60s, rhymed with my own. Around the same time, I read *Natural Right and History* (1953), by Leo Strauss, a figure often identified with neoconservatism. The German American thinker contrasted the ancient conception of rights with the mod-ern, and he made a convincing case that the moderns were in the wrong in crucial respects.

What stood out especially was his critique of modern relativism. That there are many opinions about the truth, and about right and wrong, he argued, doesn't mean that there is no truth or no right and wrong. Otherwise, "the principles of cannibalism are as defensible or sound as those of civilized life", and "nothing except dull and stale habit could prevent us from placidly accepting a change in the direction of cannibalism." Downstream from relativism (and positivism and historicism) was the unraveling of civilization itself.

This line of argument proved enormously useful to me as I navigated a law school where it was an article of faith, for example, that a poor black woman couldn't be held fully responsible for her crimes (because she was poor, African American, and therefore a victim of oppression). Though these claims were issued in the name of antiracism, they struck me as racist. They also epitomized the anticivilizational denial of moral truth and responsibility that Strauss had critiqued. If thinking this way made me a "neocon", then I was proud to be one.

Cutting against the ideological grain at my law school sharpened my polemical skills. I seemed to have a knack for formulating conservative arguments in such a way that even liberals or leftists felt compelled to listen, even if they didn't agree with my view. (Not that I was always above staking out contrarian positions and enraging polite liberal opinion for the kicks.) I also developed a healthy addiction to seeing my byline in print and to making the occasional television appearance. In short, I found my true vocation: opinion journalism.

As my final year of law school came to a close, I faced a fork in the road: I had an offer to join a large law firm in Boston, or I could work as an intern at the right-of-center opinion pages of the *Wall Street Journal* in New

York. I went with the *Journal*. Once I had my foot in the door, I hustled harder than I ever had, editing op-eds in daytime and writing my own articles on nights and weekends. I churned out book reviews, columns on foreign and domestic policy, cultural commentary, interviews, and reportage. I even subbed in for the *Journal*'s television critic.

On a balmy August day in 2012, the *Journal* hired me as a book review editor. That evening, I met a young Asian American architect named Ting at a mutual friend's apartment in the West Village. She was boisterous and charming, with long, raven-black hair, high cheekbones, and delicate features. She had none of the flighty, decadent airs of many women her age. She was serious but not self-serious. It didn't take me long to figure out why.

Ting had been born in Xi'an, China, to parents who already had a son, which meant that her very existence ran afoul of the country's one-child policy. To circumvent the law, her mother and father had fudged her birthdate and entrusted her to an aunt. It wasn't until she was thirteen years old that she was reunited with her parents, in America, where her father had found work as a professor. There was no doubt in my mind that the vitality and seriousness I observed in her, and that I found so alluring, had to do with this miraculous survival odyssey.

I had had it with random hookups and meaningless relationships. I was desperate for the stable, essentially bourgeois family life my own parents had never had. "I'm probably going to marry this woman," I told myself that night at the party. I moved swiftly to make my resolution a reality. Ting and I were engaged within the year. We tied the knot on March 14, 2014, at the New York City Town Hall. Two days later, I flew to London to take up a new post as an editorial writer for the *Journal*'s

European edition. My new wife would join me a few months later.

* * * * *

Finding work that didn't feel like work calmed my inner turmoil somewhat. Ditto for getting married. But a dishonest little split still divided my mind when it came to religion. I appreciated Christianity as a socially useful doctrine. The highest achievements of Western art, architecture, and music, I knew, all bore the stamp of the Gospels. And I personally needed the occasional visit to a church to restore my balance after my passions threw me for a spin. Yet I refused to submit to the truths of the Christian faith.

"This Christianity stuff is very beautiful, isn't it?" I would say to friends. "It's been a civilizing force, no?" But I was always careful to add: "You know, not that I take any of it to be *true*." I divided the truth and its worldly consequences. I preferred to have God without God. What was holding me back?

I had already overcome one of my main objections to belief. I used to fret about how the adherents of different religions could all be equally fervent about their respective dogmas. The Hindu believed passionately in his deities. The Muslim was equally fervent about Allah, and the Christian likewise about the Trinity. And so on. That these irreconcilable accounts of the divine could inspire equal devotion, I thought, showed either that the same Supreme Being had revealed himself in different guises to the various peoples or, more likely, that there was no divine.

But then I came across Strauss' critique of relativism and extended it to religious questions. There are many divergent accounts of divinity with equally fervent believers, I reasoned, but it could well be that one account is true while the rest are false (or half-true).

Nor was I all that exercised by "scientific" refutations of religious belief. From the Jewish bioethicist Leon Kass, I learned to distinguish science from scientism. Kass defined scientism as "a quasi-religious faith that scientific knowledge is the only knowledge worthy of the name; that scientific knowledge gives you an exhaustive account of the way things are; and that science will transcend all the limitations of our human condition, all of our miseries", as he told me in an interview for the *Journal* in 2013.

Scientists could paint a detailed picture of the origins of the cosmos, the galaxies, and our solar system. But they couldn't answer the *why* questions, the ones posed by "the fear of God and the fear of death", as Kass put it: Why did the universe explode out of an infinitely dense point some 13.8 billion years ago? Why did life emerge 10 billion years later, on a planet that orbits an unremarkable star surfing the outer edges of an unremarkable spiral galaxy? Why was there something at all instead of nothing?

These questions properly belonged to the realm of philosophy and religion, Kass insisted, yet scientism constantly tried to hijack them. It substituted facts, the product of empirical inquiry, for the *truth*, which was greater than any collection of facts. It was truth that allowed us to order facts into a cohesive view of the cosmos and of humanity's place in it. Some things could be true—spiritually true, morally true, even mystically true—yet inaccessible by empirical methods.

Scientists could describe falling in love as a biophysical event, for example, in the flow of certain hormones in the brain. But asked to define the thing itself—love—or to describe the subjective experience of it, they would come up short. For that we needed the novel and poetry and music and, yes, revealed religion. Likewise, I couldn't fully explain the healing that I experienced at the Mass in empirical terms; no one could. Yet it was real, in a mysterious way.

Then there was the force, or energy, that animated my deepest loves and longings. This force was more than my personality, and yet my personality and all of my most intuitive understandings depended upon it. It used my senses to observe the world, and yet it was more than my senses, too. It carried my happiest recollections and was also crisscrossed with wounds, new and old. Yet it was more than my memory, as well. It developed as I progressed through life's stages, yet it had remained unchanged in some fundamental way since the day I came into the world.

Well, what was this force or animating energy? *I had a soul!*

Scientism reduced all of these phenomena to neurological, psychological, and sensory realities. But again, the thing itself—the soul—was irreducible to its measurable effects. Self-reflection—and the novels of Austen, Balzac, Stendhal, Thackeray, and Tolstoy, to name but a few of my favorites—offered a far better guide to its depths than did the CAT scan or the brain map. Who could read Tolstoy's account of Prince Andrei's last days in *War and Peace*, for example, and still maintain that there is no such thing as an immortal soul?

There was a grave moral danger to scientism, as well. Though science and facts revealed a great deal about the workings of the universe, they were no guide to the moral life. They could neither account nor substitute for my conscience, the inner measure that judged my acts against a universal standard of conduct. The dictates of my conscience often (but not always) aligned with public laws and norms. Yet the conscience operated even where no human law governed and no immediate punishment awaited wrong acts. Again and again, I asked myself: "Where did this inner standard or knowledge originate? Who had put it there?"

Eventually, the only explanation I could give for these two things—the soul and the conscience—was that they were the imprints, or gifts, of a Supreme Being, the Author of a transcendent order. Yet I continued to identify publicly as an unbeliever. I was reluctant to make a full assent to the faith that already flickered in my heart.

* * * * *

God embarrassed me. The thought of worshipping him, of bending my knee in a church, was always accompanied by an inner voice that hissed: "Really now! Are you going to praise an invisible bearded man in the heavens?" On those rare, disconsolate occasions when I did pray, the same voice would mock and jeer: "There you go. You're talking to yourself again, like an old woman or a madman, and you think you're addressing 'God'. Don't you feel silly? Aren't you ashamed of yourself?"

Pride lay behind this embarrassment. For if the God of the Bible accorded with the mind as well as the heart, faith would become a personal duty, a personal covenant. I feared that I would have to relinquish my freedom—the freedom to gossip at the office, to ogle that girl in the midriff and miniskirt, to have that ruinous "one last" drink. Was I prepared for that? In the end, I answered in the affirmative. And once more, it was reading that saved me. Two books in particular helped me to see that biblical faith was not only reasonable but compelled by reason.

* * * * *

The first was *The Five Books of Moses*, Robert Alter's English translation of the Torah, published in 2004. How I came across Alter's Pentateuch, I don't remember. Probably I read a review of it somewhere and figured that it was time finally to read the Torah from beginning to end—so why not this version, which claimed to present the true syntax, rhythm, and simplicity of the biblical Hebrew as no English translation before it had?

I don't read Hebrew, so I couldn't tell you if Alter's claims about his translation had merit. Regardless, I was blown away by the beauty of these earliest pieces of Scripture, and many were the weekend mornings when I would lie sprawled out on my bed, reciting Alter's Pentateuch out loud (sometimes while nursing a hangover from the previous night's excess):

> When God began to create heaven and earth, and the earth then was welter and waste and darkness over the deep and God's breath hovering over the waters, God said, 'Let there be light.' And there was light. And God saw the light, that it was good, and God divided the light from the darkness. And God called the light Day, and the Darkness He called Night. And it was evening and it was morning, first day. (Gen 1:1–5)

The creation story, the account of the Fall, the killing of Abel, Moses' several encounters with God throughout the book of Exodus—these and other wondrous passages by turns delighted and overpowered me. And they made me question whether they were the work of human hands alone.

The genius of the Jewish people infused the text, to be sure. Nevertheless, the beauty of the language and the timelessness and universality of the substance hinted at a fount of inspiration beyond the specific historical context that had produced it. One couldn't view the Torah in the same light as, say, *The Epic of Gilgamesh* or the other scraps of mythology left over from the ancient Middle East. The

latter were of merely archaeological, historical, or literary
interest; the Torah was a living text that spoke fresh truths
across a distance of three thousand years.

Consider, for instance, God's words to Cain after Cain
murders Abel: "Listen!" says the Lord. "Your brother's
blood cries out to me from the soil" (Gen 4:10).

In a single verse, the Torah transfigured three concrete,
elemental things—blood and soil and the act of crying—
into a metaphor for guilt. For of course blood didn't cry
from soil, but the conscience was instantly aware of guilt;
it was the conscience that cried out to the Lord of moral
order. Moral order, then, preceded and informed the individual conscience. I heard the same cry every day of my
life, and so, I suspected, did nearly all people. The verse
had me saying to myself: "My God! My God! The Bible
is its own proof!"

Or take the scene of Jacob wrestling a stranger in a
twilit desert. "And Jacob was left alone, and a man wrestled with him until the break of dawn. And he saw that
he had not won out against him and he touched his hip-
socket and Jacob's hip-socket was wrenched as he wrestled
with him" (Gen 32:24–26). I recall reading this haunting
passage over and over. It had a folkloric touch that was
familiar to me as a Middle Easterner. And yet it pointed
beyond the folkloric raw material of which it was made,
toward a lucid and even frightening theophany.

Several question marks hung over this passage, not least
the identity of the "man" whom Jacob wrestles: Is he a
messenger from heaven? An angel? A "night spirit", as
Alter speculated in annotation? God himself in some quasi-
embodied form? "Not Jacob shall your name hence be
said," the stranger tells the patriarch once they stop wrestling, "but Israel, for you have striven with God and men,
and won out" (Gen 32:28). But Jacob's sparring partner

refuses to reveal his name (Gen 32:29). Jacob concludes that he has seen God "face to face and come out alive" (Gen 32:30).

The renaming of Jacob recalls Abram's rebirth as Abraham (Gen 17:5). The wrestling, meanwhile, prefigures Moses' more definitive encounters with the divine. In the Tent of Meeting, we learn, "the Lord would speak with Moses face to face, as a man speaks to his fellow" (Ex 33:11). Yet even Moses is denied a glimpse of God's face. "I shall put you in the cleft of the crag and shield you with My palm until I have passed over," God tells him in the Sinai. "And I shall take away My palm and you will see My back, but My face will not be seen" (Ex 33:22–23). God is at once friendly and near, awesome and overwhelming.

That these various passages echoed each other suggested that the Torah writers sought to convey an interconnected whole, a sequence of encounters with God that had indelibly marked the Jewish people. The literary form and the beauty of the Torah thus reflected an inner logic and gave meaning to the history of Israel.

Abraham and his progeny learn their true identity—their true name and heritage—after being initiated into a divine order. And God henceforth identifies himself as the "God of Abraham, Isaac, and Jacob". It was only in relation to God that human life attained its full meaning. "Man"—as a spiritual, philosophical, and moral concept that encompassed much more than the mere *Homo sapiens*—made sense only within a divine order of creation.

The same dialectic of mutual identification was in play at the individual level, in a way that I recognized in myself. My soul, too, wrestled with God, as it were, and sought to know his name and to be named by him in turn. Even my early "great" rebellion against God, and my quest to find cheap substitutes for him, had betrayed a longing to see God's face and to be in relationship with him. I had a soul, yes, and that soul needed God. So why not be honest about this longing!

Only, the relationship between God and man was strained, because our earliest ancestors had tried to sit in God's place (Gen 3:5). Now here was the real core of the Torah, the substantive kernel, which led me to conclude that the Bible was a truer account of human nature than any science or philosophy. Biology, psychology, sociology—none of these matched the Fall as an account of the alienation and brokenness that I felt in myself and witnessed all around me. At best, those other accounts answered the *how* questions. But the deepest diagnosis was to be found in the Bible, which said that brokenness was written into human nature, into *my* nature. I needn't have taken the story of Adam and Eve literally to agree that somehow the taint of an original transgression had spread to my own soul.

My conscience knew—and perhaps had always known—that this was true: How else to explain my predilection for doing evil for its own sake going back to the earliest days of childhood? The failure of the various utopian visions I had championed—from Marxism to the utopian liberalism of my Arab Spring days—likewise attested to the truth of the Fall. Every attempt at achieving perfect justice and liberation on human terms was bound to fail, because it would inevitably run up against fallen human nature.

No scientific discovery, no communications technology, no newfangled theory of secular salvation, no system of government, however admirable and well conceived—none of these things could ever "fix" what was wrong with the world. Sin—not "misconduct" or "aberrant behavior" or "structures of oppression" or what have you—*sin*, in the biblical sense of an affront to the divine order and a rejection of divine love, was a permanent feature of human life.

All civilizations, the pagan and the modern, felt the weight of sin. All of them, not just the people of Israel, devised various scapegoats and sacrifices to repair the breach caused by sin. That included the Shiite Islam of my childhood. It had its sacrificial lamb in the figure of Hussein, the warrior-imam who laid down his life for the truth and for his friends. All human history and all the best art and literature through the ages and across nations told this one story: of the inexorability of sin and the yearning for sacrificial expiation.

* * * * *

The Bible, however, told an additional story: that of God taking it upon himself to repair the damage wrought by the Fall. I didn't begin to grasp this other story until I read *Jesus of Nazareth*, the first book written by the German theologian Joseph Ratzinger after he was elected the 265th pope of the Catholic Church. It was to this one book, more than any other, that I owed, and still owe, my soul and my salvation.

I bought *Jesus of Nazareth* shortly after Benedict XVI's 2008 visit to the United States. I watched television coverage of the visit, and I remember thinking that this was a very holy man. Yet it took me a year to crack it open and another couple to make it through a relatively short text, in part because my knowledge of the Bible was still spotty, and *Jesus of Nazareth* demanded a basic familiarity. Still, I often studied it in conjunction with Alter, which meant that I read the Torah with Benedict, and I read Benedict's analysis of the New Testament in the light of the Old.

On one level, *Jesus of Nazareth* took on the various strands of theological liberalism that sought to cast doubt

on the historicity of the Jesus portrayed by the four evan-
gelists. To answer the skeptical theologians, the pope went
on a "personal search for the face of the Lord". The result
was a sophisticated theological polemic that also served as
a Christian primer addressed by a loving pastor to his flock
and to a God-starved West.

At the heart of the book was that same Great Reversal—
the Highest switching places with the lowest and submitting willingly to humiliation—that had so affected me
when I had read the Passion narrative in Matthew all those
years earlier. Benedict taught that the Great Reversal had
begun not at Calvary but at Bethlehem, that it was there
all through Christ's public ministry. He also showed how
nearly everything in the Old Testament pointed toward
precisely this Great Reversal, toward the Word becoming
persecuted flesh.

Et incarnatus est. What a marvelous, what a mind-
boggling idea! The Incarnation overturned every "natural" picture that man had of God. Its very improbability
to my mind counted in its favor: The omnipotent subjects
himself to weakness; the Tent of Meeting becomes the
manger; the Ark of the Covenant, a lowly Virgin; the creative Word of God, a newborn (with all the vulnerability
that that implied); the pillar of smoke, the wood of the
Cross. God is spat upon, scourged, crowned with thorns,
and executed in the most humiliating fashion imaginable.

It was all too strange, too radical, to be man-made.

Reading the Bible as a unified whole, as Benedict urged,
revealed the continuity between these two apparently
contradictory conceptions of God. There was one narrative arc bridging the Old and New Testaments, and that
was God's drawing ever nearer to humanity and revealing
ever more of himself. This drama of divine self-disclosure
culminated in a forgotten corner of the Roman Empire a

little more than two thousand years ago, when God—the same God of Abraham, Isaac, and Jacob—entered history in human form and revealed what he had denied even to the prophets: his face.

That face looked like love, the bloodstained face of the Son of God. The face of the Lord was "crucified love", as Benedict put it. Bloodstained and crucified, because only the self-sacrificial love of God could make right what was crooked in human nature. Thus, Jesus was not just a great man come to preach harmless moral maxims à la Confucius. Jesus was not a political liberator come to end hunger in Africa and Latin America. Jesus was not a liberal rabbi come to ease up Jewish ritual. Simply put, Jesus was God, come to bring God and reconcile man to him.

As I approached the final pages of *Jesus of Nazareth*—I couldn't pinpoint the exact moment—I decided that this was the truest account of God and man and the relationship between the two.

I had already accepted the Fall as the most penetrating account of what ailed the world and me. I felt the Fall to be real as sure as I felt the pain of a pinprick or the thirst of dehydration. I saw its effects in all of my failings. I could almost touch the grime that encrusted my soul from years of my own lousiness. My *conscience*, then, was telling me something. Indeed, it had been whispering and then yelling it for quite a while. And it happened that the message of my conscience was in concord with the Christian faith as expounded by Benedict XVI. Who else but the self-sacrificing God-Man could set right what had gone wrong in the Garden?

None other. Nothing and no one else worked. Only Christ Jesus.

The world, and my own cynical side, had long tried to drown out that message with the opposite idea: "Relax. Be

reasonable now. You can live a good, moral life without
the superstition of religion. If you want to honor Christianity's historic contributions, by all means, try to catch a
performance of Rachmaninoff's *All-Night Vigil*. Watch
a movie by Andrei Tarkovsky. Go admire some Caravag-
gios at the Met. You can be 'enriched' by Christianity
without going whole hog. You're enlightened, remember.
You're *roshan-fekr*, an intellectual."

Benedict XVI thundered against such complacency and
relativism, against this "dictatorship of convention":

> Does someone achieve blessedness and justification ...
> because he has declared his opinions and wishes to be
> norms of conscience and so made himself the criterion?
> No, God demands the opposite: that we become inwardly
> attentive to his quiet exhortation, which is present in us
> and which tears us away from what is merely habitual and
> puts us on the road to truth.

On the plane of politics, the worldly, "reasonable", do-
as-you-like-without-God alternative always led to slavery.
One form of this temptation promised to fill every belly
so long as man cashiered God. That was Marxism, and it
wrought "ruin and destruction even of the material goods",
as Benedict noted. Another form of the temptation was
"the worship of well-being". That was the temptation in
advanced technological nations. Left unchecked, the appetite for "rationality" and "well-being" could lead to a dysto-
pian society of the abortion clinic and the euthanasia facility
and the test-tube baby. Think *Brave New World* instead of
Nineteen Eighty-Four.

Even as I hailed "free people, free markets" as a *Journal*
editorial writer, a revulsion was growing in me of market
democracies that lacked an absolute authority to say no to

their sins. I especially feared efforts to bring the mysterious dimensions of life—birth, love, sex, death—under man's full, scientific dominion. Western democracy was magnificent, yes, and I wouldn't choose to live under any other model, at least in the fallen here and now. Only democracy didn't obviate—but heightened—the need for those "steadying brakes" that Koestler had written about.

Too much autonomy was as likely to yield despotism as the hideous statist projects of the last century. True freedom, Benedict taught, was something else. It was "freedom in the service of the good", freedom that allowed "itself to be led by the Spirit of God". To know what God wants and to bring oneself into conformity with the transcendent order of the universe, then, *was freedom*. That was the essence of Israel's joy, what set it apart from the pagans with their idols and god-emperors. The Christian, however, had the added joy of knowing the "face" of the law: self-sacrificial love. The road to the fullest freedom ran through the Cross.

By the time I was thirty years old and settled in London, I saw all of this clearly. I would even voice some of it privately, among a few close friends. Still I was in no rush to ascend Calvary.

CHAPTER TEN

THE HOUSE ON THE CAPE OF OLIVES

The boy's socks reeked of urine and excrement. Probably he had stepped onto the squat latrine neglecting to wear the communal slippers. In his restless slumber, he would fling his feet in my direction every few minutes, almost always landing a kick on the crown of my head.

Ten of us lay side by side on the floor, in two neat sardine rows. The boy with the fetid feet slept in the spot above mine. I had no choice but to suffer his kicks in silence. Crawling sensations on exposed skin hinted of an insect infestation, but the room was too dark, and the invaders too fast, to pinpoint the exact species. Cigarette smoke hung heavy in the frozen air. There weren't enough blankets to go around; those who had managed to get their hands on them were wrapped like mummies; the rest shivered. Outside, the hollering of drunks and the booming of fireworks announced the new year, 2016.

I couldn't fall asleep if I tried. I had managed to gain entrée to an Afghan smuggling ring in Istanbul, and I was about to tell the story of the European migrant crisis from the inside, as no Western reporter had or could. Unlike most of my journalistic rivals, I spoke Persian, the second language of the migrant trail (after Arabic), and I could fit in with these poor souls. A career-defining triumph was at hand. I pictured myself signing a lavish book deal and, later, delivering an acceptance speech at some journalism awards ceremony.

Fear mingled with these happy thought bubbles. My adventure could go very wrong, very fast. As often as the boy kicked at my head, I would reach inside my peacoat, which I was using for a blanket, to feel for a hidden pocket. There, wrapped in several layers of duct tape, was my U.S. passport, the thin legal tissue that set me apart from the others. An authentic Western passport went for several thousand euros on the black market. I shuddered to think what might happen to me if one of my travel companions found the document.

Or if the smugglers discovered that I was a journalist rather than a bona fide client. At the very least, I would be kicked out and be forced to restart the project from scratch. And what would become of Alireza, the Iranian migrant who had brought me here? Alireza had neither time nor money to spare. He was a man on the run. I felt responsible for his fate.

* * * * *

A friend of a friend of a friend had introduced me to Alireza a few days earlier, after I put out word on Iranian social media that I was looking to accompany a migrant on the journey from the Middle East to western Europe. We spoke by WhatsApp while I was in London and Alireza on a bus heading from Tehran to southeast Turkey. He agreed to let me join him on one condition: Under no circumstances were the smugglers and other "travelers" to know that I was a reporter.

"We'll say you're my cousin," he said. "Otherwise everything will go to rot. Capisce?"

"Understood," I replied. "We can say we're cousins who grew up apart."

"You got it, brother. Bring two thousand dollars. Cash. And pack lightly. You don't want to be too heavy on the water. Ha ha ha!"

Alireza was due to arrive in Istanbul on New Year's Eve. I flew there from London. From Istanbul onward, we would travel together. The plan was to make a series of illegal crossings that would take us from Turkey's western shore to the Greek isles, then through mainland Greece and the Balkan States, until we would reach Germany, the migrant Zion. Known to journalists and officialdom as the Western Balkan corridor, this route had brought more than a million newcomers to Europe by the end of 2015.

The new arrivals included people fleeing the infernal wars in Syria and Iraq, as well as Afghans, Iranians, Pakistanis, Bangladeshis, and many others who saw a chance to escape the misery and precariousness of life in their homelands. This mass exodus was made possible by highly efficient smuggling networks that operated like any large enterprise but for that their clients and commodities were human beings. I traveled to Turkey to tell this story.

* * * * *

Taksim, the bustling square around which the rest of Istanbul orbits, was buried under half a foot of snow when I got there. A festive mood reigned in the nearby tangle of shops, tourist bars, and hotels. Couples snapped selfies by snowmen. Burly restaurateurs carved doner kebabs, tempting the crowds with a greasy respite from the frigid temperatures. Stylish young women walked arm in arm, giggling and casting flirtatious glances at passing groups of young men. Syrian children slid down the ice-covered asphalt, making do with cheap sneakers for sleds.

A lonesome Turkish Santa imitated Father Christmas' signature laugh, poorly: "Ho-ha-he!"

My nerves were shot. I walked over to an Irish pub
and ordered a double Jameson, neat, and a Kronenbourg
to wash it down. Alireza wasn't answering my calls and
messages. Had he been detained at the border? The mutual
friend's friend who had made the connection was an Iranian dissident. Was Alireza a political case, too? In any
event, my cell phone eventually rang. It was him; the
snow, not Iranian border guards, had delayed his bus.

He told me to come to the "Usman Peh-leese". I
couldn't make heads or tails of this, so I headed in the
direction of the Atatürk monument at the center of Taksim. There were only two hours left in the year, and hundreds of young people—Turks, Arabs, Iranians—were
milling about the monument in anticipation of the count-
down. Their various nations were at each other's throats
over Syria, but here, they mixed and made merry under
the steely gaze of the Father of Turks—the same gaze that
had brought me such comfort all those years earlier at the
Turkish-Iranian border.

I had no clue what Alireza looked like. I circled the
monument a few times, searching for an unfamiliar face in
the throngs. Then I figured it out. "Usman Peh-leese" was
the Ottoman Palace hotel, on the southern edge of Taksim. And there he was at the entrance, dressed in an Adidas
athletic jacket with matching pants and bright orange running shoes. He was tall and broad shouldered and looked
as if he had struggled to fit his muscly bulk into his clothes.
His equine face broke into an easy smile when he spotted
me, unveiling two rows of large, gapped teeth.

I suggested that we head to my pub to get our bearings.
We needed to get in touch with Ehsan, our smuggler. Alireza's phone was almost out of battery power, so he used
my UK cell to make the call. He told the man on the other
end—it was unclear whether it was Ehsan himself—that he

was borrowing a British tourist's phone. It was the first of many times that Alireza lied as he did something that could have endangered both our lives: bring a reporter into the inner sanctum of a smuggler. He covered his tracks with heaps of *ta'arof*, the beguiling Persian art of affected deference and self-effacement. We were instructed to take a taxi from Taksim to a neighborhood called Zeytinburnu.

"Oh, one more thing," said Alireza as the call came to an end. "Remember I mentioned my cousin who wants to get on the water. Is there still room for one more?"

There was room for one more. Now there was no excuse for backing out of this.

Alireza negotiated hard at the cab stand, but the inclement weather made it a seller's market, and we had to settle for a gouging fare. The swirling lights and hubbub of Taksim faded into slushy darkness as our taxi made its way through the city's less touristy precincts, toward Zeytinburnu. By then the infusions of liquid courage had left me more than a little buzzed.

If Alireza was nervous, he didn't show it. He spoke Persian in the *looti* vernacular of the south Tehran working class. The tone and cadence were such that, no matter the substance of his speech, he sounded as though he were vaguely objecting or taking issue—with his interlocutor, with the world, with God. "South Tehran" was more than an accent or a sensibility. It was a whole constellation of situation ethics, street wisdom, and survival skills, all of which Alireza appeared to possess in spades.

In the backseat of the taxi, he recounted a life story laden with misfortune. He had been born to a poor and pious Muslim family. His athlete's physique, and arms and fists made for punching, had propelled him from those humble origins to the kickboxing semipros by the time he was a teenager. Yet his talents had come to naught, and he was a broken man before he decided to try his luck on the migrant trail. At thirty-two, he was only a year older than I was.

The source of his worldly misfortunes was his conversion to Christianity. Last time Alireza was in Istanbul, in January 2015, he and a dozen other young men had been baptized in the name of the Father, the Son, and the Holy Spirit at a ceremony organized by one of the many Turkey-based Protestant groups that cater to Iran's underground evangelical scene. When they flew back to Tehran, security forces arrested them at the airport. A regime mole had infiltrated the group of converts. Alireza was detained for days.

"Sir, I didn't know what I was doing," he had blurted at one point, as an interrogator slapped his face over and over. "I love Islam! My life for Islam! My buddies told me this was to be some sort of water-therapy deal!"

The interrogator had burst out laughing at this; the beating went on.

"When they start hitting you," Alireza recalled, "you'll say anything to make them stop."

He would go on to deny Jesus several more times before the authorities released him. Afterward, the railroad company where he worked fired him. He took up odd jobs—construction, fruit picking, scrap metal recycling—but couldn't make ends meet. The neighborhood boys stopped showing up for the kickboxing classes he taught out of the makeshift gym in his apartment. He considered taking his own life. When word spread that Germany had flung the gates open to migrants from the Middle East, he borrowed enough money from relatives to pay the smugglers and took off.

"The me that left Iran was a corpse," he told me. "You know, in Iran, Mother is something else. How could I leave my mother behind? Brother, I dragged a corpse out of that house." But he wouldn't change anything if he could go back in time. "With Islam, it's 'You're a Muslim, or we kill you.' With Christianity, there is a real choice, a real touch of God. That's what I have."

A real touch of God. His Christianity was as simple as that. Too much so, I thought, and I was inclined to doubt his faith on account of its simplicity. Then it occurred to me that, with his Baptism, Alireza had bound himself to Christ in a way that was infinitely more concrete and meaningful than my bookish half faith could allow. I still only admired the Cross from a polite distance. This simple man had thrown himself at its foot. For him, faith in Jesus Christ was as natural and effortless as being awe-struck by lightening. He was my Ivan Denisovich.

A silence fell between us. Then the taxi driver's gruff voice jolted us back to the present. "Address?" he asked. "Address!"

"Mister, I want please your phone," Alireza replied in a broken English.

It was time to get exact directions, and we couldn't use my foreign cell a second time lest Ehsan get suspicious. The driver obliged. Alireza dialed Ehsan's number on the driver's phone and handed it back. Soon driver and smuggler were chatting away in Turkish. Before long, the car came to a gentle stop on an empty road, next to a gated parking lot. "Migros," the driver grunted. "This, Migros!"

Next to the parking lot was a sign for a supermarket, the only source of light for a mile around. Migros, read the orange letters. This was Ehsan's meeting spot. Alireza tried to haggle again, but the Turk was having none of it. We paid up grudgingly. Though it appeared desolate on New Year's Eve, we were, in fact, standing next to the main thoroughfare at Zeytinburnu. The Turkish name, I would later learn, meant "Olive Cape".

"It's a good thing we only paid thirty lire for that ride," Alireza said as we exited the cab.

"We did?" I replied. "I thought it ended up being eighty."

"No! Remember? We only paid thirty."

Alireza didn't want the "others"—meaning the other travelers—to think we were saps. Or that we had extra lunch money.

"When we get there," he said, "let me do all the talking. You don't say a word, even if you're asked a direct question. Got it? Be cool."

I wasn't cool. My mouth felt like sandpaper. I lit a cigarette. Alireza didn't smoke. Five silent minutes passed beneath the Migros sign, but there was no sign of Ehsan. Then a whitish figure emerged out of a dark alley that ran perpendicular to our main road, and before we knew it, he was standing in front of us. He was probably no taller than five-foot-six. His slanted Afghan eyes, small pursed lips, and sinewy neck exuded vigor and malice.

"My brother!" Alireza said, a wide grin crossing his lips. "I kiss your tired hands for waiting up for us so late." Again, the *ta'arof.*

The other didn't reciprocate Alireza's affability. "I thought you were supposed to be alone," he said. His glare could cut glass.

"Don't worry, my friend," Alireza said, with a hint of a plea in his voice, not that the power dynamics needed clarifying. "Ehsan knows all about him. This is my cousin. Ehsan knows. Ask him." So *this* fellow wasn't Ehsan.

Without another word, the other swiveled in his spot and started back toward the alley from where he had come. He was almost jogging. We followed. I was breathless.

Midway, the Afghan turned around and made a lighter gesture at me. I fumbled through my pockets and produced what he wanted. He didn't say thanks. We arrived at Ehsan's house in short order.

* * * * *

That was how I ended up spending New Year's 2016 with Afghan migrants and the smugglers who held the keys to their European dreams.

Dawn broke on January 1, and light from a distant winter sun fluttered through the curtains. I sat up in my spot. I hadn't slept a wink. I glanced at my nighttime tormentor. He was about fourteen, judging by his size and the peach fuzz above his lips, yet his chubby features and long hair betrayed a certain girlishness. Two other Afghan boys were lying on their backs nearby. Though they were probably about the same age as the first, these two looked rougher and older, more feral. The tough who had greeted us with such warmth and hospitality the previous night wasn't far, either.

The room was perhaps 150 square feet, and it crawled with cockroaches. These were half an inch long at most, much smaller than the urban roach. Yet what they lacked in size they made up for in sheer numbers. There was at least one and usually many more in each spot that my eyes rested upon. Some raced across the walls, as if competing in some Cockroach Derby. Others milled about languorously, over the blankets, atop the television in one corner, on the bodies and faces of the dozing travelers.

"Man, I nearly froze to death," Alireza said. He was up.

"I froze, too," said an old man sitting squat two spots down from Alireza. He was bald, with a leathery sunbeaten face and no front teeth.

"Really?" I chimed in. "I was kind of warm." I lied to appear hardened.

The whole room was now animated with men's morning activity. Those who had slept with blankets folded them neatly and piled them in one corner, a quaint gesture toward Middle Eastern fastidiousness amid the filth that engulfed us. We made a valiant but futile effort to shoo away or kill some of the roaches. Then we sat in a semicircle around the television. All the Afghans lit cigarettes, including the trio of boys. I followed suit. Alireza still abstained. Someone turned on the television and flipped through the channels until he found a figure-skating broadcast. No one objected to the sight of a young girl in a short frilly skirt spinning gracefully.

"Is this happening right here, in Turkey?" asked one of the boys.

"Yeah, it's actually right next door," answered another. "When she's done with her routine we can go congratulate her, and you can ask her out."

"Hardy-har-har."

"Is this a woman or a doll?" asked one of the men. "I mean, how can a woman look *this* perfect?" He was short with a round face and a thin mustache. He wore an impossibly unfashionable mullet haircut. His thin arms and legs contrasted markedly with his fat belly.

"When you get to the other side, brother," said Alireza, "you'll get yourself a sweetheart just like her."

"How can a woman look so much like a doll?" the other repeated himself, as if in a reverie. "My God. My God." Then he turned toward Alireza and me: "Are you gents heading to Germany?"

"God willing," Alireza said.

If they managed to cross the Aegean, most of these travelers would likely end up in Germany or Sweden, the two countries that were most eager to accept the newcomers. Yet the travelers themselves passionately debated where to settle once they made it to mainland Europe, almost like a family weighing various vacation destinations.

A consensus formed around Britain, mainly because most of them spoke at least a little English. But the travelers also knew that the crossing from France across the Channel was no easy feat. Canada was nice, too, but they had to make it to Europe first and then pay a smuggler an additional $20,000 to hide them aboard a trans-Atlantic vessel. Finland was "too cold, and they don't pay much welfare", one of the guys said. Switzerland was too expensive. Alireza mentioned that he had considered trying for Australia but had decided otherwise after he learned that the authorities diverted illegal boats to Papua New Guinea.

"There are so many darkies down there it makes you puke," he said. "Imagine having to share a hot cell with a darky. Yuck!"

I checked for my passport. It was still there.

"It's like that in Turkey, too, if you get caught," said the bald old man. "They'll dump you in a cell with the Syrians and the darkies. But then they'll release you a few days later. You can always try again."

This old man claimed to have spent more than half of his life on various smuggling runs. He had crossed illegally from Afghanistan to Iran numerous times while hiding in the narcotics-stuffed undercarriages of buses and trucks. In the 1990s, he had tried to cross from Turkey to Greece and from southern Iran to the Emirates; he had been caught both times.

"Migration itself is a form of jihad, children!" he said, guffawing to reveal his toothless gums.

"Speaking of which," Alireza said, "when is this Mr. Ehsan coming here?"

The room went silent. Then the tough spoke up for the first time: "How would we know? Maybe later. Maybe he isn't coming. Maybe he's sitting among us."

"Don't you work with him?"

"Nah. I'm just a traveler. Like you." Ah, so he was putting on airs the night before, pretending to mind the smuggler's safe house.

"And what do you call yourself, brother?" Alireza asked, his affability now shaded by a hint of threat.

"Nader," the other replied before turning to the group: "Anyway, what do you gents wanna eat? I'll go pick something up."

The travelers ordered a sumptuous feast: eggs, cream, cheese, kebabs. But on a budget of one lira per capita, they would have to settle for a more modest breakfast. I chipped in my lira, dreading the prospect of sharing a meal with the cockroach army that swarmed the room. There was no choice, however. If I acted as effete as I really was, it would raise suspicion among the others. A traveler is supposed to be famished at all times; to pass up a full meal is a sure mark of insanity.

Nader and one of the feral boys—they were related, I gathered—returned a few minutes later with a frying pan filled with eggs over easy. Too easy, in fact. Nader set the pan in the middle of the room, and his younger assistant passed out bread rolls to the rest. All sat squat around the pan and began dipping their rolls into the eggs. Alireza cupped one hand around his eggy roll and rammed it whole down his throat, inhaling it in one bite.

"Mif-ter Foh-rab!" he said in a muffled voice between chews. "Come inject fome of thif good-neff right into your veinf!"

I had to do it. I took a small piece of bread and dipped it gently into the slippery mess. I would slowly nibble at the bread to give the impression that I was eating without actually consuming much. I would help myself to the Clif Bars in my backpack once I found a moment away from the others.

Meanwhile, an argument broke out between the boys as the men scraped the bottom of the pan. I couldn't be sure what was said (the Afghans spoke in their own dialect when they weren't addressing Alireza and me, the two Persians). I think one of the feral boys attached to Nader had joked about throwing the third boy—the feminine-looking one who had kicked me through the night—into the water during the crossing, and this latter had come back with a sexual epithet.

Nader, who had been listening attentively the whole time, suddenly picked up the near-empty pan and hurled it with great force at the epicene youth. The pan crashed into the wall next to him with a deafening sound. It barely missed the boy, though he caught much of the oil and slop. Shock froze him in place. Nader lunged at him and was about to smack his face with an open palm when the bald old man jumped up and arrested his arm midmotion. The boy cowered into a corner of the room.

"Mr. Nader," the old man said, "I beg you. This boy is traveling alone. He doesn't have anyone in this world. He's learned his lesson. Please don't punish him anymore. He won't dare insult your cousins ever again. I beg you! Now, let's all say a *salavaat*. Come on, gentlemen!"

At this, we all stood and chanted the familiar Arabic words: "Allah's blessings be upon Muhammad and the progeny of Muhammad!"

* * * * *

At noon or a little after, Ehsan arrived to meet the latest cohort of clients. Nader had kept us under lock and key until then, claiming that he was under orders from Ehsan to make sure none of us left the safe house. It was possible that he had such instructions but more likely that he enjoyed lording over others and had installed himself as hall monitor for the purpose.

Alireza and I were summoned to Ehsan together. The smuggler's office, in a small bedroom next to ours, reminded me of a sort of hippy's lair, with a Persian carpet covering the floor, a guitar on a stand in one corner, a bird's cage in another. The smell of burning incense filled the air. Ehsan sat cross-legged in the middle, dressed in a tie-dye T-shirt and skinny jeans. He had a Bruce Lee haircut and pronounced Central Asia features. A green warbler balanced its thin legs on his shoulders, and Ehsan now gently shifted his torso and now petted the bird to discourage it from flying away. The warbler's chirping supplied a pleasant soundtrack.

The smuggler motioned for us to join him on the floor. Quite unlike my mental impression of an Afghan criminal, Ehsan was friendly and polite. He spoke in a silvery voice, and an inscrutable smile remained planted on his lips the whole time. It turned out that the point of this meeting was to upsell us on additional services beyond the basic boat ride to the Greek isles. If we paid him $8,000 each on top of the agreed $2,000 for the Aegean crossing, his men could get us from Athens all the way to Paris or Berlin or wherever else we wished on the mainland, all by car, saving us the hassle of trekking on foot and by train.

"Mister! Mister!" Alireza interrupted Ehsan's sales pitch. "We don't have that kind of money. We just want to get to Greece. We'll figure it out on our own."

"As you wish," said the smuggler. His bird flapped its wings and zoomed over to its open cage.

"So ... what do we do when we get there?"

"Simple. You stop being Iranian and become Afghan war refugees. Iranian is no good for asylum."

"No good, huh?"

"Well, it's much better to be an Afghan." Ehsan peered deeply into Alireza's eyes, and continued: "Hmm, you might have some trouble. Your Iranian-ness is printed on your face. But you're not too hopeless. Just come up with a good Afghan story. Learn your Afghan geography. The brothers in there can help." At this, he tipped his head in the direction of our room.

"As for you," he continued, now turning to me, "you're good. You'll pass."

You'll pass. For the first but not the last time, I was reminded that I was closer to these men than I would have cared to admit. It was only by dint of birth and circumstance that I had a U.S. passport, while they had to risk the waters of the Med aboard unseaworthy vessels to get to Europe. *You'll pass.* The words created a sinking in my soul that stayed with me long after I parted ways with the smugglers and the migrants.

* * * * *

We spent the rest of the day watching corny Iranian soap operas from the prerevolutionary days and anxiously awaiting word from the smugglers about our crossing. To send a dinghy across, water conditions must be calm. The coast must be clear of Turkish border patrol. And there have to be enough travelers to maximize profits for the smugglers.

The stars aligned for our group the next day, and we were told to get ready. In the evening, a van would take us from Istanbul to Izmir for a crossing at dawn on January 3. The news set off a flurry of activity among the travelers. We now needed to shower and clean up, waterproof our belongings, and purchase life jackets (though I had brought a professional one from London). Someone also mentioned buying honey and lemon juice, the drinking of which was supposed to counteract hypothermia in case our dinghy capsized and we found ourselves in the winter water.

Alireza and I left to buy him a life jacket, and we offered to pick up the honey and lemon juice for the group. Mullet man—he was called Morteza—joined us as we stepped outside for the first time in thirty-six hours. Ehsan's apartment was on the first floor of a three-story building, in an alleyway strewn with bricks, plastic garbage, and other detritus of working-class life. The surrounding area was thick with impoverished Turks and, Morteza claimed, the kinsfolk of Uzbek, Kazakh, and other Central Asian fighters waging jihad against the Assad regime in Syria.

Travelers overran the streets, especially the market, where every shop seemed to hawk life jackets, waterproof gear, duct tape, plastic bags, and other migration essentials. Alireza quickly settled on one of the more top-of-the-line life jackets on offer. At seventy lire, it might have assuaged the wearer's fear of the water, but it wouldn't save his life in a pinch, since it lacked a flotation mechanism. But even that model was too fancy for Morteza, who had to buy jackets for himself and several of the guys at the house. He couldn't afford to spend more than thirty lire per jacket.

The Afghan took us on a circuitous tour of the market, as he tried on every possible model and haggled with every salesman. By then memory of the passport in my pocket had partially receded from my mind, and I found myself oddly absorbed in this drama. Again the thought crossed my mind that I could have easily switched places with Morteza, for whom even a toy life jacket was out of reach.

After an hour's bargain hunting, Morteza finally settled on a life jacket. As we were leaving the market, however, a trio of young girls approached us. They were dressed in yoga pants that left little to the imagination, and their fake lashes and glossy makeup stood out sharply in a neighborhood where burkas and *jalabiyas* were common, and where at midday we had seen worshippers praying in the streets and sidewalks near the local mosque for lack of room inside.

"Excuse me," said one of the girls to Alireza, "do you speak Persian?" They were Iranian.

"Yes?"

"Do you know how we can get to ——?" Here she named a neighborhood none of us had heard of.

"Truth be told, we're travelers here, too. Maybe a taxi, but I've heard there are buses—"

"Oh, really? 'Cause we're new here, too!"

"Right. Well, we wish you success. God be with you."

"Listen, you wouldn't happen to have a room for us, would you? We'd love to stay with you for a while." At this, she took a step closer to Alireza and twirled her cheap hair extensions around a finger. The proposition came so fast that I didn't even catch it in the moment. What struck me, instead, was that hidden beneath the caked-on makeup was the face of a girl-woman, no older than fifteen or sixteen. Alireza declined the offer cheerfully, with lots of *ta'arof* and expressions of regret.

Afterward, Morteza explained that he had witnessed scenes like that several times since he had arrived in Istanbul: "Before you two sirs arrived, we ran into a couple of them, and just like these three they offered to stay with us. Of course, we had no room. But would you believe it, not a minute after we turned them down, some Turks rolled up in a Beamer and picked them up. They were young girls. Children made up like dolls! Like dolls . . ."

* * * * *

The men were showered and in high spirits when we returned in the late afternoon, life jackets and honey and lemon in tow. An arduous journey still lay ahead. Yet for the Afghans, the hardest part—crossing through the icy mountains of northwestern Iran, where the border guards had shoot-to-kill orders—was already behind them.

Alireza and I set about waterproofing our clothing, wallets, cell phones and chargers, and the rest. I caught glimpse of a Persian-language New Testament among Alireza's belongings, though he was quick to hide it away.

Nader, the tough, was missing. Having waterproofed and squared away my stuff, I went over to the boy who had almost had his ears boxed the day before.

"What's your name?" I asked.

"Behnam," he replied.

"You all right?" I asked him.

No, he nodded his head up and back.

"Well, you're going to be in Europe soon. Doesn't that make you happy?"

No, he gestured again.

"Do you regret coming here?"

"I had a good job in Iran," he said. "I swear, I did. I kept a rich man's house in Tehran, and he paid good money. All I needed was papers. I should have stayed there."

"Why did you come?"

He shrugged. Because he could, I suppose. Or because everyone was doing it.

"What's the score, Mr. Sohrab?" Nader's voice gave me a jump.

"The score?" I replied. "I'm not sure what you mean. What score?"

"The score, man! The score! What are you, dense?"

"The score's ten-zero!" Alireza intervened. "Never mind Mr. Sohrab, brother. He's my cousin, but he's a bit of a fancy-boy. Grew up uptown. Doesn't speak our tongue."

All Nader was asking was "What's up?" But I didn't catch the slang.

"Aha," Nader said, considering this for a while. "And how's my little kitten doing?" he asked, now turning to Behnam.

The boy was silent—and visibly frightened.

"Come on!" Nader went on. "Kitty, kitty, kitty! Give me a meow!"

He was humiliating the boy.

"Meow," Behnam said meekly. "Meow. Meow."

"That's better. And how does the little kitten clean himself when he's dirty?"

Behnam stopped meowing.

"Do I need to give the little kitten another beating?"

Now the boy started mock-licking his hands and arms, indeed like a cat.

"Good. Now come on, little kitten. Come help me cook dinner."

Nader disappeared into the kitchen. The boy followed him dejectedly.

When they returned half an hour later, we set out a picnic blanket on the floor, swept cockroaches and bread-crumbs from the surface, and sat in a circle around it. Nader and Behnam had prepared fried potatoes and onions in the Afghan style. The leftover rolls from the morning were handed out, and we dove in. I was famished. I inhaled the potatoes much as Alireza had done with the eggs at breakfast. I didn't mind the cockroaches any longer.

"Man!" one of Nader's cousins exclaimed. "Behnam makes a good kitchen maid, doesn't he?"

"Hey!" the old man said. "Don't speak to him like that."

"I'm just joking," answered the offender.

"If you can't make nice jokes, please don't joke."

"I'm just saying he's a good little bitch. Maybe you can cook for me in Europe, too, Narges dear?" (Narges is a woman's name.)

Behnam whacked his bully with a still-full melamine bowl, drawing a scream. The two were about to tangle when Nader grabbed Behnam by the collar and pinned him against the wall. Having immobilized the boy, Nader jabbed his elbow into his face, hard. Once. Twice. Thrice. The boy cried out in pain. The rest of us were powerless to rescue him—that is, except for the professional kick-boxer. Alireza cleaved apart the two entangled bodies; then he put Nader in a headlock for a few moments till reason returned to him.

Ehsan stood at the doorway with his arms crossed. The warbler on his shoulder chirped. "None of you will get on the water if that happens again," he said calmly before retiring to his office.

Behnam collapsed as soon as he was freed from Nader's grip. His face was red, and swollen like a chipmunk's, and he lay on the floor for some time whelping and whimpering while the rest of us finished dinner. His persecutors had finally reduced the boy to an animal state.

"Now, now, gentlemen," said the old man. "Let's say the *salavaat* and put this behind us."

"Allah's blessings be upon Muhammad and the progeny of Muhammad!"

* * * * *

I never crossed the water with that group of travelers. An hour after the brawl, I got a call from the United States informing me that my mother, now living in the suburbs of Boston, had been hospitalized with an epileptic episode. I told Ehsan and the others that I needed to fly home to Tehran, to take care of my mother, which was almost true. All were quite sympathetic. Nader even embraced me when we said farewell. I never saw any of the travelers again, though I later received word from Alireza that they had all made it safely to Germany.

My time in Ehsan's safe house shattered what was left of my faith in perfectibility and progress and the bland secular universalism that is the lingua franca of Western elites. Human nature was so much more unfathomable, and horrible, than all that. There, in that shabby corner of working-class Istanbul, I discovered a portal to the lower depths of human misery. Ehsan's house was a kind of charnel pit or Sheol, though the people in it were yet alive. It was a void, though it existed within the boundaries of space and time. It was on fire with degradation—and sin.

How to escape those flames, which had set the whole world of men ablaze ever since that first betrayal in the Garden? That was the only question that mattered to me, really, after I parted ways with the smugglers and migrants.

My father had urged me to be myself, and every philosophy that I had tried on since then stood for the same idea in different guises. But my pure "self", without more, was insubstantial and purposeless and interchangeable. It lacked a metaphysical home and destination. If what I saw and heard in Ehsan's house disturbed me, it was only because the goings-on there reflected, in externalized and concentrated form, my own miserable spiritual state. The fires brushed and penetrated my soul. The smoke grew thicker and the searing flames rose higher with each passing year.

There was only one escape hatch that led out of the infernal prison in which my soul was trapped, and it happened to be cruciform in shape. The only way out was through the One who so loved the world that he descended from the austere heights of Sinai down to these lowest depths, who called slaves friends, who allowed himself to be degraded and lifted up again as the paschal Victim for all ages. I had already accepted the truth and necessity of faith in Christ Jesus before I came to Istanbul. The house on the Cape of Olives warned me that there was no time to waste. I, too, had to throw myself at the foot of the Cross without delay.

CHAPTER ELEVEN

FROM FIRE, BY WATER

When my mother recovered, I returned to London with a spiritual zeal such as I had never before exhibited. My two decades as an atheist now appeared for what they were: squandered years, during which I had turned my back on God and neglected my immortal soul. The realization was cause for trembling, yet it also brought great joy: the joy that comes with perceiving the proper order of things, with exercising spiritual muscles long atrophied, with fresh murmurings of prayer and mystical understanding in the heart.

Life had taught me that our Lord's gift of radical absolution on the Cross was the only thing capable of repairing the brokenness in me and around me. Jesus was the God-Man, who came to take away the sins of the world (Jn 1:29), and all that was graceful in the West flowed from this one truth. Yet his agonized call from the Cross echoed in every soul, not just the Western. Indeed, Christianity was the precondition of true universality and true brotherhood. But for the Son's sacrifice, men remained alienated from the true Father (Jn 14:6), and therefore from each other.

Yet the mansion of "mere Christianity"—faith in Jesus as the only Son of God—had many rooms, as C. S. Lewis had written in his little book of that title. Which room, which communion, was I supposed to pick? Be

careful, Lewis warned, not to choose a room for superficial reasons. Rather ask: "Are these doctrines true? Is
holiness here? Does my conscience move me toward this?
Is my reluctance to knock at this door due to my pride,
or my mere taste, or my personal dislike of this particular
doorkeeper?"

My romance for Catholicism persisted, and I owed my
whole Christian mentality to Benedict XVI and his *Jesus
of Nazareth*. Even so, I stood for a time in the doorway
of evangelicalism and admired that room. Then I turned
away, walked through the door marked "Rome", and
never looked back. My decision turned precisely on the
question of liturgy, which Lewis had dismissed as a superficial matter. In the Roman room, I found worship that
conformed fully with the truth of Christ's identity. I redis-
covered the Mass.

* * * * *

My flirtation with evangelicalism had begun before that
fateful trip to Istanbul. Soon after I moved to the United
Kingdom, in 2014, I came across a British activist, about
my age, who advocated for persecuted Christians in the
Middle East. At a gathering of dull Tory types in a rooftop bar in Covent Garden, Miles Windsor stood out for
his wry, wicked sense of humor and movie-star looks; he
was a dead ringer for Brad Pitt. In between wisecracks,
he spoke fearlessly about his evangelical faith among
people who were, at best, indifferent to faith.

That metaphysical indifference, so pervasive in England
and the rest of western Europe, I now found positively
revolting. I had come far from that boyhood dream of secularity. Human beings were created for more, and needed
more, than endless consumer choice and kaleidoscopic
lifestyles. But for many of my well-educated, well-to-do

friends in London and New York, lifestyle-ism—clean eating, mindfulness, banana treatments—was all they had. Out of these lifestyles, some more lascivious than others, they had fashioned idols. So much for secularity.

Miles' faith was an oasis in this barren spiritual landscape. We hit it off right away, not least because he had a tattoo on his arm that read, in Persian, "Free Farshid." Farshid Fathi was a born-again pastor imprisoned in Tehran for the "crime" of evangelizing and possessing Persian-language Bibles. Miles had dedicated himself to rescuing Fathi, and the Iranian pastor's name was etched on his skin as a daily reminder of the price that Christians in the Middle East pay for fidelity to the Nazarene. Now here was a true heir to William Wilberforce.

He became my go-to source on the persecuted Church in the Middle East. Thanks to Miles, a letter from Fathi to his followers, written during Christmas 2014 and smuggled out of prison, made its way into the pages of the *Wall Street Journal*. "Although the beauty of Christmas … cannot be found in this prison," the letter read, "with the ears of faith I can hear the everlasting and beautiful truth that 'the Virgin will conceive and give birth to a Son, and they will call him Immanuel.'" Those words stayed with me long after the editorials were forgotten.

Soon the journalist-source relationship developed into a friendship—my first genuine Christian friendship. It was at Miles' suggestion that I began a regimen of daily Scripture reading. It was to him that I first intoned the words "I accept Jesus Christ as my Lord and savior." He kept inviting me to Sunday services at his church at Wimbledon, no matter how many lame excuses I made. When, a couple of years later, I returned from Istanbul with that burning vision of Sheol-on-earth, my first thought was to ask Miles and his Anglican vicar about a Baptism.

But I didn't go through with it. I figured I would first attend a few more Anglican services—to inspect the room, per C. S. Lewis—before taking the plunge. My wife and I were living in West London at the time, and I gathered from Miles' vicar that the nearest "sound" Anglican church— meaning evangelical and conservative-ish—was Holy Trinity Brompton, or HTB, as it was popularly known.

Located in tony Knightsbridge, roughly equidistant from Harrods department store—that playground of wealthy Russian émigrés and Gulf Arabs—and the Victoria and Albert Museum, HTB was the most influential evangelical institution in Britain. The Anglican communion's cultural and theological fault lines ran right through the Regency church, which, with its elaborate stained-glass windows and vaulting arches, played host to charismatic worship that included JumboTrons, rock bands, and funky lighting.

The first HTB service I attended kicked off with a rendition of "Our God Is a Great Big God", a praise song that compared Almighty God with a skyscraper ("He's higher!"), a submarine ("He's deeper!"), and the universe ("He's wider!"). Kids and adults alike raised and swayed their arms at the skyscraper bit, and they held their noses, shook their bottoms, and dove "underwater" at the submarine bit. The rest of the musical numbers were less childish but equally saccharine.

The pastors, fresh-faced men and women who all appeared to have walked out of a J.Crew catalogue, peppered their sermons with biblical citations, and there was no denying their faithful enthusiasm. None of the sermons was memorable, however, and if one were to boil away the personal anecdotes and other extraneous bits, all of them could be distilled into the following: *We have been saved. How blessed we are for that! So continue to develop a personal relationship with Jesus. Amen.*

That was it. The sermons touched on weighty questions—salvation, the centrality of Scripture, how to relate to our Lord—but the touch was all too light. The uplift was real enough, and I remember walking out of that first service, and several subsequent ones, with a gladness in my heart that would color the rest of my Sunday. But the joy would dissipate come Monday, and I was left with an emptiness. There was something wrong.

Evangelical Protestantism, for all its Spirit-infused hand raising and arm swaying, struck me as profoundly abstract. Under the evangelical dispensation, the only point of contact, so to speak, between the Christian soul and the divine order was Scripture and preaching based on Scripture. A "personal relationship" built on words alone, even divinely inspired words, was incomplete. Our Lord and his disciples preached, yes, but they also did other things, supernatural things, and these were missing altogether at HTB.

Then, too, the preaching itself was weak sauce. There was a copy-and-paste quality to it: a little bit of Daniel here, an allusion to Revelation there, some Matthew over here, and so on, all too often in service of a palliative or self-affirming message. There was nothing like the systematic biblical vision that I had found in Benedict, who, for example, could illuminate the true meaning of the Beatitudes (as our Lord's revelation of himself as the "new Torah"), all while parrying blows from Nietzsche, Marx, and the like.

Of course, it wasn't fair of me to compare young evangelical pastors with one of the greatest theologians of the twentieth century. Yet I couldn't help but detect the problem of *authority* in the Protestant orbit, which, I came to suspect, lay behind Protestantism's theological shortcomings. At that point, mind you, I had yet to recognize the authority of the Catholic Church—though, as my weeping over Benedict's photo showed, I was instinctively drawn to Catholic authority. But in early 2016, my attraction to Catholic authority was strong enough that I sensed the fragility and thinness of authority among Protestants.

That, in turn, raised an even more troubling concern, having to do with the nature of the church. If all that mattered was pursuing a personal relationship through Scripture, then why have a church at all? Why couldn't each person go it alone? I posed this question to more than one Protestant in those days, and all offered some variation on the following: The church exists to strengthen fellowship among the faithful. We help each other grow in faith, and "where two or three are gathered in my name, there am I in the midst of them" (Mt 18:20).

That answer never satisfied me, yet I couldn't articulate why until I encountered *the* Church.

And what about sin and salvation? It was the mystery of evil and the reality of the conscience that had compelled me to assent to the Christian faith in the first place. Afterward, I couldn't square the "reformed" notion that I was already saved with my sin-racked conscience, which told me the opposite. Salvation by faith alone, which evangelicals trumpeted at every turn, ran counter to common sense and, taken to its logical terminus, led to predestination without free will. That didn't seem right, either.

It was, finally, the cheesy, irreverent worship that most contributed to my turn away from evangelicalism. This was worship conformed to the tastes of bourgeois British (and American) families circa 2016. It reduced cosmic truth to a Top 40 sensibility, which I couldn't abide. Still I continued to attend services at HTB, from time to time. These were good, earthy people. The Word of God was at the center of their lives. And Catholics didn't exactly send me text messages asking: "Would you and your wife like to join us for Sunday service?" Evangelicals did.

* * * * *

One Sunday morning, as I was making my way home from the nine-thirty service at HTB, I spotted a sign posted at the entrance of the Catholic church next door, known as the Brompton Oratory. I had walked past the graying neo-baroque edifice countless times before, but this was the first I paid any attention to it. The sign advertised a "Solemn High Latin Mass" for Pentecost Sunday. The Mass was to start at eleven o'clock. I was just in time.

It was dark and refreshingly cool inside. Kneeling worshippers packed most of the pews—remarkable, given that the nave trumped even Saint Paul's Cathedral for size. Much as I had done all those years earlier at the Capuchin monastery in Manhattan, I sat in one of the back pews. Only this time, I was dumbfounded by the beauty all around me. I have visited numerous Catholic churches in Europe since then, but the London Oratory is second to none for balancing classical grandeur and intimate Christian emotion.

My eyes were drawn down the nave to the sanctuary and high altar, as the architect no doubt intended. At the top, under a protective canopy, was an engraving of the Immaculate Heart of Mary, from which shone gilded rays of light. Just beneath was a painting of Saint Philip Neri, the great sixteenth-century Roman holy man and founder of the Oratorians, kneeling rapt before a vision of the Virgin carried by clouds and surrounded by angels and cherubim. Staging and surveying this scene, high above the clouds, were God the Father and the Paraclete dove.

Marble covered the whole apsidal space: onyx, scarlet, serpentine, red-and-yellow breccia and other kinds, all matched so harmoniously that none seemed out of place. The altar, made of white marble, stood out against this colorful medley. Six large candles topped it, with a golden crucifix in the middle, which in turn led down to the tabernacle. A little porthole window off to the right of the apse concentrated a jet of sunlight from the outside onto the crucifix and the tabernacle—the illumined nexus, where the Trinitarian glories above met the people below.

This was a holy place, set apart from the banality and corruption of human affairs. It was a place of right worship. Its beauty was the work of human hands yet transcendent in effect. Here, beauty paid an enduring homage to the theological precepts that inspired and preceded it. And if metalwork and masonry and painting directed my imagination to spiritual realities, was that not because Almighty God had blessed me with a receptive imagination in the first place?

The Mass itself reinforced and quickened this line of thinking. A bell rang. All stood. The choir chanted the *Asperges me.* Though I didn't understand all of the Latin, my heart registered perfectly the thirst for God and his mercy in the psalmist's words. The retinue of priests and deacons made their way down the aisle. I remember wishing that a drop of that holy water might reach me. It wasn't to be, and this only heightened my thirst for the sacramental life that it symbolized. *Asperges me, Domine, hyssopo et mundabor ...*

Order. Continuity. Tradition and totality. Confidence. These were the watchwords my mind conjured for itself as I threw myself into the Mass. When the congregation knelt, I knelt. When the people crossed themselves, I followed suit, though more than once I did it with my left hand, which drew a sharp look from the rather haughty young man next to me. I didn't mind. The Catholic Church was already making demands of me. I was called to conform myself to a body two millennia in continuous existence, not the other way around.

The world was unimaginable without the Catholic Church. Whereas if one day the earth swallowed up HTB or any of the other thousands of Protestant churches that pop up annually, it would be a great tragedy—but not a world-historical one. The institution that appeared fusty and antique was timeless and universal, a fortress against the ephemeral. The one with JumboTrons and rock 'n' roll was small and parochial, a pure product of its age. These differences had to mean something.

A middle-aged priest delivered a homily on the Holy Spirit in the Church. How seamlessly and intelligently he wove the day's readings together with his reflections on the Church and the world in our time! Again, the word that crossed my mind was *confidence*: The Catholic Church didn't need to bend herself to the vacuous fads of 2016. She taught and offered the same thing she had from the beginning. She *was* the same thing. And what was that? God, in a word. God in his Word—and in corporeal form.

Lewis had been wrong to write off "style of worship" as a secondary matter in *Mere Christianity*. As with beauty and imagination, the order and symbolism of public prayer were bound up with truth. The Mass gave full expression to the truths and mysteries of Christianity. The Cross was there, but so was our Lord's crucified body, with the pierced side, the bloodied hands, the scourged and welted back, the thorns cutting into the forehead. His sacrifice was present. And so was the Virgin, who had given him flesh from her own flesh, nursed him from her bosom, and accompanied him to the last. She was our link to the Incarnation—how could we leave her out of worship?

I savored the Mass of the Faithful, and when the people lined up at the altar rail to receive the Blessed Sacrament, I positively envied them (I knew enough to know that non-Catholics are barred from taking Communion). It was nearly unbearable to recall that I had spent a third or more of a lifetime worshipping idols—the idol of "history", the idol of "progress", and above all the idol of self—when the true God was this gentle, this self-giving. *Domine, non sum dignus, ut intres sub tectum meum: sed tantum dic verbo, et sanabitur anima mea.*

The Mass lasted an hour and twenty minutes. I was sorry when it was over. Before exiting, I walked over to the Sacred Heart chapel at the back of the church and knelt at the prie-dieu facing a statue of our Lord. This was an utterly spontaneous act of obeisance, unmarred by hesitation. I had found God in his Church; indeed, the two were coterminous. But what was I supposed to say to him? I had yet to memorize the necessary prayers. The words that came to my mind were: *Forgive me. Cleanse me.* I must have repeated them thirty or forty times before I got up and left.

Forgive me. Cleanse me. Forgive me. Cleanse me.

The following Monday, on my way to work at London Bridge, I got off at the South Kensington stop on the Underground and raced on foot to the Oratory House. An old priest opened the door halfway when I knocked. He was short, dressed in an elegant black cassock with the signature Oratorian collars sticking out at the neck. His metal-rimmed glasses and protruding ears accentuated his bookish, wizened expression.

"Yes, how may I help you?" he asked in a strikingly posh English accent.

"I wish ..." My voice was shaking. "I wish to become a Roman Catholic."

The priest didn't miss a beat: "Very well. I shall instruct you."

* * * * *

So began my period of instruction with Father R.C.J. We met each Sunday afternoon beginning in June 2016. He asked very few questions, and there was very little room for discussion. I wouldn't have had it any other way. This was catechesis, not a dialogue. We didn't need to play icebreaker games or make colorful posters or whatnot. And what, really, did I have to say to the Church that she needed to hear? Nothing. At our first meeting, he did inquire about my background and why I wished to become a Catholic.

All I could muster was something about "the majesty, er, magisterium".

Father saved me from myself: "Right, the majestic magisterium, let's say." Then he proceeded to teach for about an hour. "We begin with Saint Thomas Aquinas. Order in nature and natural theology ..."

* * * * *

Father R. and the Oratory epitomized an English Catholicism, which, precisely because it had suffered half a millennium of repression, ostracism, mockery, and finally indifference, was all the more rigorous and vital than the soupy and fast-secularizing Anglicanism that encircled it. This was the pungent Catholic culture that had formed such converts as John Henry Newman, Henry Edward Manning, and Ronald Knox, among others, and a whole constellation of literary stars, including G. K. Chesterton, Robert Hugh Benson, Evelyn Waugh, and Graham Greene.

My catechist was himself a convert and a spiritual son of one of the greats, Monsignor A. N. Gilbey (1901–1998),

that eccentric icon of twentieth-century English tradi-
tionalism. Heir to the Gilbey gin fortune, the monsignor
won fame for converting numerous young men at Cambridge while serving as the university's Catholic chaplain.
He also waged a valiant campaign to stop the chaplaincy,
Fisher House, from going co-ed; the doors were opened
to women in 1956 anyway.

He retired that year. The liturgical changes that accompanied Vatican II the following decade came as another
blow. He withdrew from public preaching and spent his
last years at the Travellers Club on Pall Mall, where he
was allowed to maintain a chapel in his room. His private
Masses attracted the Catholic literati, and every few years
the *Spectator* would dispatch a scribe to profile the cleric
seemingly teleported to our age from Victorian times. Gilbey played the part with aplomb: "I don't believe one man
one vote is a sort of moral law!" "There you go again with
this absurd idea that Christianity says all men are equal. It
says nothing of the sort!"

Gilbey was also a man of deep faith and a Catholic
thinker in his own right. As Father R. told it, Gilbey's
whole mission in life was, quite simply, to put others on
the path to heaven. "Dear boy, dear boy," Father would
quote his mentor, "the best is yet to come!" To that end,
Gilbey had agreed to have his commentary on the old
"penny" Catechism, which had won so many young men
for the Church at Cambridge, recorded and transcribed.
The 1986 book that came about as a result made the best
sellers list, to the monsignor's own surprise.

It was this book, *We Believe*, that formed the basis of
my instruction. It presented Catholic dogma with tremendous clarity, without subtracting one iota from its richness.
Gilbey's synthesis provided a theological grounding to
the sweet, docile feelings about the Church, which I had

nursed for a decade. More important, Gilbey showed how eminently reasonable Catholicism was—such that, once my course was finished, I couldn't fathom how others called themselves Christian without submitting to Rome's light yoke.

All of those teachings of the Church, which posed as stumbling blocks to her critics, were, in fact, sensible, biblically sound, part of a cohesive whole, whose elements fit together with logical perfection. This realization I owed, above all, to Father R. and to his legendary mentor.

Start with *the authority of the Catholic Church*. To believe in God, it sufficed to rely on natural reason alone, as I had done. But to go further with him, as it were, it was necessary to believe divine revelation on the authority of the Revealer. And there was nothing wrong with accepting things on authority. As Gilbey put it, "We ought not to make heavy weather about doing in our relationship with Almighty God what we do daily in our dealings with other people"—that is, to accept all sorts of propositions solely on authority.

And the whole of revelation turned on a single proposition: namely, that the Catholic Church was Christ's supreme revelation. Assent to Jesus Christ thus meant assent to the Church he founded and the powers he granted her, chiefly to forgive sins (Jn 20:23; Mt 16:19) and to teach all nations (Mt 28:19). Scripture and Tradition confirmed all this, yet the Church didn't need to appeal to these things for her authority. Before Scripture or Tradition existed, the Catholic Church was there at the Cross and the Resurrection.

Another stumbling block: *the development of doctrine*. Purgatory. The Immaculate Conception and the Assumption. Papal infallibility. Weren't these Romish distortions of an "original" Christianity? "No!" thundered Gilbey. While the Church occasionally adopted new vocabulary and concepts to expound her teachings, the truth of Christ's revelation remained unchanged. The monsignor went on to offer decisive proof from Scripture and Tradition for each of these doctrines, yet he never conceded that Rome was *required* to proffer such proof. Again, it was enough that the Church *was* "Christ in corporate form".

Still another: *the centrality of the Blessed Virgin*. Far from a Roman eccentricity, devotion to Mary was the "touch-stone of orthodoxy". Without Mary, Christianity risked losing the truth about Christ's own identity—the union of two natures, divine and human, in one person—and drifting toward Gnosticism of various kinds. On this point, and on love of Mary more generally, I required very little persuasion. That I even had a shot at eternal salvation, it seemed to me, was made possible by the free consent of a Jewish Virgin of the Galilee.

Finally, the biggest stumbling block of all: *the Real Presence of Christ in the Eucharist*. Here, Gilbey marshaled an abundance of data in favor of the Catholic teaching about the Blessed Sacrament and the supernatural action at the heart of the Mass.

There was, of course, the Bread of Life discourse in Saint John's Gospel. Our Lord, when confronted with his followers' doubts about the Eucharist, doubled down: "Unless you eat the flesh of the Son of man and drink his blood, you have no life in you" (Jn 6:53). He insisted that he was speaking literally, whereas elsewhere he was quick to clarify that he was speaking figuratively (cf. Jn 3:1–5). So much of Jesus' public ministry, moreover, involved nourishing his followers with food and drink, acts that prefigured the Eucharist and revealed the link between the Real Presence and the Incarnation. Then there was the evidence from history. To wit, when early Christians worshipped, they had the Mass and the Eucharist. Bible study groups, these gatherings were not.

In the end, however, it wasn't reading that brought me to faith in the Real Presence but the Mass. Observing the reverence with which the Oratorians celebrated the sacrifice, and the awe with which the people received the Victim, did far more to stoke my appetite for our Lord's Eucharistic presence than any theological discourse. Mass after Mass, I watched as others took Communion, and all I wished to do was to lie face down on the ground before the Sacrament in abject adoration. There was no better proof of his presence than this desire. And if the Real Presence was true, then whatever else Rome taught had to be obeyed. In the end, then, I became Catholic because I concluded that Catholicism *was* Christianity in full, while other forms of Christianity were digressions from this fullness.

* * * * *

My period of instruction would prove among the most grace filled of my life. At the outset, I ordered a vintage prie-dieu and had it installed in a corner of my room, under a reproduction of Velázquez's *Christ Crucified*. This setup became the focal point of my nascent and ecstatic spirituality. Nothing made me happier than the time I spent kneeling before that sublime image of the bloodied and dying Jesus. This, even though the substance of my contemplation was sorrowful. Constant joy-in-sorrow, another Catholic paradox.

I also developed something like a plan of life, which involved morning prayers followed by reading Scripture and studying a portion of the 1992 Catechism. I learned to say the Angelus from Father R., and the prayer came to frame my day, culminating in the six o'clock Angelus that

preceded the weekday evening Mass at the Oratory. If he
had imparted nothing else—and he taught me a great deal
more—I would remain forever indebted to Father R. for
inculcating in me this habit of "retreating to the hermitage
within" three times a day at the Angelus.

Spiritual reading filled the in-between-work hours. In
addition to *We Believe*, Father R. lent me a copy of Monsignor Knox' *The Creed in Slow Motion*. Published in 1949,
the book gathered a series of lectures on the Apostles'
Creed, which Knox had delivered to a group of Catholic schoolgirls taking shelter in the countryside during
the Nazi bombing of London. Under those conditions,
Knox had called on the girls to live lives of "gracious
fanaticism"—the pithiest definition of saintliness I ever
came across.

There were many other books, but the ones that proved
most formative included *Death on a Friday Afternoon*, Richard John Neuhaus' meditation on the Seven Last Words
of Christ; and the *Apologia* of Newman. The latter wasn't
particularly enjoyable, as far as spiritual autobiographies
go, yet, like *We Believe*, it was one of those books that
lent order and coherence to feelings and intuitions I had
long entertained, and I was grateful to be able to say, after
Newman, "Aha! So I'm far from first to have felt this feeling or thought this thought!"

Thus, Newman on the pivotal role of imagination in
Catholicism: "[Rome] alone ... has given free scope to
the feelings of awe, mystery, tenderness, reverence, devot-
edness, and other feelings which may be especially called
Catholic." Or Newman on the conscience as proof for
God and the Catholic faith, which he, like Gilbey, identified as almost one and the same thing: "I am a Catholic
by virtue of believing in a God; and if I am asked why I
believe in a God, I answer that it is because I believe in

myself, for I feel it is impossible to believe in my own existence (and of the fact I am sure) without believing also in
the existence of Him, who lives as a personal, All-seeing,
All-judging Being in my conscience."

But no book I read in those days surpassed *The Confessions* of Saint Augustine. How I had gone thirty-one years
without having read *The Confessions*, I couldn't tell you.
Had I read it earlier in life, the Bishop of Hippo would
have saved me a lot of trouble and misery. I had stumbled
through most of life up to that point, drunk on the errone-
ous notion that what is new is best, while *The Confessions*
was the greatest testament, after the book of Proverbs, to
the truth that nothing fundamental changes in the affairs
of men.

Including error. All false doctrines, Augustine said,
seek to negate man's responsibility for sin. The astrologers
whom he glommed onto in his youth tried to "excul-
pate man, 'flesh and blood' (Mt 16:16; 1 Cor 15:50), that
proud putrefaction, and to blame Him who created and
ordained the sky and the stars." Couldn't the same have
been said for our latter-day astrologers, who cast the blame
for sin on economics (Marxism), on "repression" (liberalism), on the unconscious (psychoanalysis), on Dead White
Males (identity politics), on language itself (structuralism
and post-structuralism), and so on?

This fourth-century North African seeker had waded
through the same river of error as I had! In the end he
had concluded that "there is no rest where you seek it.
Seek what you seek but it is not where you seek it." That
sentence could have served as the epitaph on my grave-
stone, had I died before knocking on the door marked
"Rome". I owed him something more—and could
have depended on him for more—than a few pages of
notes in my reading journal. When Father R. told me to

think about a patron saint, I didn't hesitate to respond: "Augustine."

* * * * *

Father R. never ceased to remind me—gently, subtly—that the sum of Catholic knowledge was infinite, and whatever I knew or thought I knew amounted to a miniscule share of the whole. After six months of instruction, however, he determined that I was well formed enough to be received into the Church (prior to that, when I pressed him about a date for my Baptism, he would say only, "When you're ready"). On December 19, 2016, I was to be baptized and confirmed. I would also take my First Communion and have the archdiocese convalidate my civil marriage. Four Sacraments in a single day.

"When that water is poured," he said at our last meeting before the big day, "you become truly initiated into the life of Christ—into Trinitarian life. Say to yourself, 'I live no longer as I but Christ lives in me.'"

"And afterward?" I asked.

"The best thing I can do for you after I baptize you is to shoot you."

"Straight to heaven, eh?"

"Yes, well ..." Short of dying right after Baptism, the best course was to attend daily Mass, make frequent use of the Sacrament of Confession, and live by our Lady's admonitions at Fatima: Love. Pray. Suffer. Repent. The journalist and the peasant girl alike were called to do the same things. Only, one of the two was luckier than the other, for it required her far less intellectual striving to accept these teachings.

* * * * *

Thick clouds smothered London in the days leading up to my Baptism. My body felt heavier than usual, as if pressed by the urban smog. The night before, I dreamt that I was in a strange urban complex—a dreary sort of transport hub–cum–shopping mall on the outskirts of a strange city. Someone directed me to a private locker room hidden in a subterranean corner of this complex. Inside was a glass tank in the shape of a cube, filled with pristine water. Just as I began to inspect the tank, a drop of blood fell into the clear liquid, and the single red particle instantly spread through the whole volume, turning the water a bright crimson like the sky at dusk . . .

I woke up drenched in sweat. The rest of the day had a similarly phantasmagorical quality. Then with a dash of water Father R. broke my fever. *You'll pass*, the smuggler from that house on the Cape of Olives had said. Yes, but my deliverance would come by other waters—waters mingled with blood most precious.

Benedictus Sanguis eius pretiosissimus.

END

ACKNOWLEDGMENTS

The joy of joining the One True Fold is beyond the power of words to relate. Yet this memoir attempts to relate some of that joy, as well as the corresponding terror of tip-toeing at the edge of Sheol. If I have achieved any measure of success at either task, it is thanks to the Author of every grace; every shortcoming is mine alone.

The book wouldn't see the light of day were it not for the support of many others, to whom I am deeply indebted. The first to suggest that I write about my conversion were Damian Thompson and Dan Hitchens of the *Catholic Herald*. Dan would go on to serve as my godfather when I was received into the Church. In him I have found a true and loyal friend—a rarity later in life—and an exemplar of Christian tact and gentleness.

Father Joseph Fessio and Mark Brumley of Ignatius Press offered to publish my memoir, saving me the agony of writing a proposal and shopping it around. I thank them and their colleagues Vivian Dudro, Laura Peredo, Anthony Ryan, Diane Eriksen, John Herreid, and all of the other Ignatius team members for their dedication to the project and a painless editorial process. Thanks as always to my agent, Keith Urbahn of Javelin Literary.

Archbishop Charles Chaput is a courageous soldier for Catholic truth and orthodoxy. I am immensely grateful to His Excellency for his generous foreword and to his assistant, Francis X. Maier, for making it possible. His Eminence Raymond Leo Cardinal Burke, Professor Robert P.

George, Kathryn Jean Lopez, and George Weigel likewise have my heartfelt gratitude for their kind endorsements.

Numerous friends helped with the manuscript or otherwise kept me company through the lonely writing process. Ann and Neil Corkery took me on an enchanting Roman pilgrimage in July 2017, and Father Roger Landry was a most excellent chaplain and guide in the Eternal City. Chad C. Pecknold of the Catholic University of America, my one-click-away theologian, and Charlie Huenemann, my old philosophy professor, shared their feedback on crucial passages. David Gallagher ran his eagle eyes over the whole manuscript, saving me much embarrassment. *Muchas gracias* to Monsignor Javier García de Cárdenas—pastor, teacher, and friend.

I would be remiss if I didn't thank my friends Father William Dailey, Brian Finnerty, William McGurn, Robert Nicholson, David Propson, Rusty Reno, Benedict Rogers, Matthew Schmitz, and Andrew T. Walker for the spiritual and intellectual nourishment they provided me.

There are three men to whom I owe my career in journalism and whom I have resolved to thank in every book I publish till I pass from this earthly vale. They are James Kirchick, John Podhoretz, and Bret Stephens. To John, Abe Greenwald, Noah Rothman, and the rest of my former colleagues at *Commentary*: Thank you for letting me join your grand adventure. Keep the candle burning.

Last but not least there is my wife, "my path to heaven", Ting. The writing of this memoir coincided with the birth of our son, Maximilian. Ting bore all of the pressures of new parenthood with love, patience, and grace, allowing me the time and space needed to write the book. Wife of my youth, I fall in love with you a little more with each passing day. Here's to eternity.

FURTHER READING

Nietzsche, the Existentialists, and the Existential-ish

Burroughs, William S. *Naked Lunch*. New York: Grove, 1992.

Camus, Albert. *The Myth of Sisyphus*. Translated by Justin O'Brien. New York: Vintage, 1991.

———. *The Plague*. Translated by Stuart Gilbert. New York: Vintage, 1991.

———. *The Stranger*. Translated by Matthew Ward. New York: Vintage, 1989.

Dostoevsky, Fyodor. *Notes from Underground*. Translated by Richard Pevear and Larissa Volokhonsky. New York: Vintage, 1993.

Hesse, Hermann. *Siddhartha, Demian, and Other Writings*. New York: Continuum, 1998.

Ionesco, Eugène. *Exit the King*. Translated by Donald Watson. New York: Grove, 1978.

Kafka, Franz. *The Complete Stories*. New York: Schocken, 1995.

———. *The Trial*. Translated by Willa Muir and Edwin Muir. New York: Schocken, 1992.

Kierkegaard, Søren. *Fear and Trembling, Repetition*. Translated by Howard V. Hong and Edna H. Hong. Princeton, NJ: Princeton, 1983.

Nietzsche, Friedrich. *Thus Spoke Zarathustra: A Book for All and None*. Translated by Walter Kaufmann. New York: Modern Library, 1995.

Sartre, Jean-Paul. *No Exit and Three Other Plays*. New York: Vintage, 1989.

Marxism, Freudianism; Post-Marxists, Post-Freudians

Baudrillard, Jean. *America*. Translated by Chris Turner. New York: Verso, 1989.

———. *Simulacra and Simulation*. Translated by Sheila Faria Glaser. Ann Arbor, MI: University of Michigan Press, 1994.

Foucault, Michel. *Madness and Civilization*. Translated by Richard Howard. New York: Routledge, 1994.

Freud, Sigmund. *The Basic Writings of Sigmund Freud*. Translated by A. A. Brill. New York: Modern Library, 1995.

Lacan, Jacques. *Écrits*. Translated by Bruce Fink. New York: Norton, 2007.

Lyotard, Jean-François. *The Postmodern Condition: A Report on Knowledge*. Minneapolis, MN: University of Minnesota Press, 1984.

Marx, Karl. *The Eighteenth Brumaire of Louis Bonaparte*. New York: International Publishers, 1998.

———. *The German Ideology*. Amherst, NY: Prometheus Books, 1998.

———. *Wage-Labour and Capital, Value, Price and Profit*. New York: International Publishers, 2001.

Marx, Karl, and Friedrich Engels. *The Communist Manifesto*. Translated by Samuel Moore. New York: Penguin, 2002.

Trotsky, Leon. *Their Morals and Ours*. New York: Pathfinder Press, 1973.

Political Awakenings

Havel, Václav. *Living in Truth*. Boston: Faber & Faber, 1990.

Kass, Leon. *Life, Liberty, and the Defense of Dignity: The Challenge for Bioethics*. New York: Encounter, 2004.

Koestler, Arthur. *Darkness at Noon*. Translated by Daphne Hardy. New York: Scribner, 2006.

Manent, Pierre. *Beyond Radical Secularism: How France and the Christian West Should Respond to the Islamic Challenge*. Translated by Ralph C. Hancock. South Bend, IN: St. Augustine Press, 2016.

————. *Democracy without Nations? The Fate of Self-Government in Europe*. Translated by Paul Seaton. Wilmington, DE: Intercollegiate Studies Institute, 2013.

Sharansky, Natan. *Fear No Evil: The Classic Memoir of One Man's Triumph over a Police State*. New York: Public Affairs, 1998.

Strauss, Leo. *Natural Right and History*. Chicago: University of Chicago Press, 1999.

The Beginning of Wisdom

Alter, Robert. *The Five Books of Moses*. New York: W. W. Norton, 2004.

Augustine. *The Confessions*. Translated by Philip Burton. New York: Everyman's Library, 2001.

Benedict XVI, Pope (writing as Joseph Cardinal Ratzinger). *Introduction to Christianity*. San Francisco: Ignatius, 2004.

————. *Jesus of Nazareth: From the Baptism in the Jordan to the Transfiguration*. New York: Doubleday, 2007.

Gilbey, A. N. *We Believe: A Simple Commentary on* The Catechism of Christian Doctrine Approved by the Archbishops and Bishops of England and Wales. Leominster, Herefordshire, England: Gracewing, 2011.

The Holy See. *Catechism of the Catholic Church*. New York: Doubleday, 2003.

Knox, Ronald. *The Creed in Slow Motion*. New York: Sheed & Ward, 1949.

Lewis, C.S. *Mere Christianity*. New York: HarperOne, 2015.

Neuhaus, Richard John. *Death on a Friday Afternoon: Meditations on the Seven Last Words of Jesus from the Cross*. New York: Basic, 2001.

Newman, John Henry. *Apologia Pro Vita Sua*. New York: Penguin, 1995.

INDEX

Abraham, 161
Ahl al-Bayt, 40
Ahmadinejad, Mahmoud, 151
Ahmari, Sohrab. *See also*
American life; childhood and
family in Iran; conversion;
education; intellectual life
and development; journalism,
career in; religion; Teach for
America
Baptism, 191–92, 206–7
birth, 33
drinking and alcohol consump-
tion, 104–5, 118, 139–44,
146, 171
drug use, 92, 106, 118, 144
marriage, 154–55, 206
Middle East and Islam, working
theories about, 149–52
New York weekend, 138–47
alcohol. *See* drinking and alcohol
Alexander the Great, 27
Ali ibn Abi Talib, 40, 41
Alireza (guide), 169–87. *See
also* European migrant crisis,
reporting on
Alter, Robert, 158–63
American life, 70–85
as aspiring intellectual, 81–85
education in, 73, 74–77, 79,
81–84
emigration process, 43–44,
66–69
English and American
vernacular, 70–71, 75
first creative efforts in, 82
Iranian life contrasted with,
136, 149
Iraq War, U.S.-led, 111,
132–33
misapprehensions regarding,
70–71
9/11, 83, 111, 149
poverty, experience of, 77–79
relations between sexes in,
75–77, 81
religion in, 70, 71, 73, 79–82
social critique of, 72–74,
81–83, 91–92, 102
sports and athletics in, 73–74
in Utah, 71–74
American/Western culture
childhood attraction to, 21–23,
44, 64–66, 67, 81
Iranian revolution (1979) and,
28
Muslims living on fringes of,
149–50
role of religion in, 136–47,
155, 189
Westoxication or
Weststruckness, 66, 68
Amis, Kingsley, 22
Angelus, 203–4
Angelus Novus (Klee), 108
Anglicanism, 192